GOD'S LAW MADE EASY

GOD'S LAW MADE EASY

A Made *Easy* Series Book

Kenneth L. Gentry, Jr., Th.D.

VICTORIOUS HOPE
PUBLISHING

Chesnee, South Carolina 29323
"Proclaiming the kingdom of God and teaching those things which
concern the Lord Jesus Christ, with all confidence."
(Acts 28:31)

Kenneth L. Gentry, Jr., Th. D.
New edition (c) Copyright 2020 by Gentry Family Trust udt April 2, 1999

The Made *Easy* Series from Victorious Hope Publishing provides substantial studies on significant issues in a succinct and accessible format from an evangelical and Reformed perspective.

Printed in the United States of America

ISBN 978-1-7343620-2-2

Victorious Hope Publishing
P.O. Box 285
Chesnee, SC 29323

Website: www.VictoriousHope.com

Scripture quotations are taken from the New American Standard Bible®, Copyright © 1960, 1962, 1963, 1968, 1971, 1972, 1973, 1975, 1977, 1995.

Dedicated to
Rev. Kenneth G. Talbot, Ph.D.

Friend and Scholar

TABLE OF CONTENTS

ABBREVIATIONS

BAGD   F. Wilbur Gingrich and Frederick W. Danker, A *Greek-English Lexicon of the New Testament and Other Early Christian Literature* (2d. ed.: Chicago: University of Chicago Press, 1979).

LC   Larger Catechism

OED   *Oxford English Dictionary*. Oxford: University Press.

WCF   *The Westminster Confession of Faith*

ANALYTICAL OUTLINE

Chapter 1

INTRODUCTION

Our Current Predicament

We live in an age of accelerating moral decline which bodes ill for the future of our culture, society, and nation. A stable, peaceful, and productive society requires a clear, secure, and righteous moral foundation. Man cannot exist without a moral code to restrain his sinful passions and to guide him to righteous conduct. A tragic lament that closes the book of Judges bewails Israel's moral confusion which led to her social chaos: "Every man did what was right in his own eyes" (Jdgs 21:25; cp. 17:6). This problem exists today.

Our currently collapsing mores are especially a deep concern for Christians because "if the foundations are destroyed, / What can the righteous do?" (Psa 11:3). Providentially, Christianity originally took root in the soil of the *pax Romana*, the great Roman peace that allowed extensive road building and the free flow of communication. Hence, Paul encourages prayer for civil authorities, partly so that the faith might grow more easily:

> First of all, then, I urge that entreaties and prayers, petitions and thanks-givings, be made on behalf of all men, for kings and all who are in authority, in order that we may lead a tranquil and quiet life in all godliness and dignity. This is good and acceptable in the sight of God our Savior, who desires all men to be saved and to come to the knowledge of the truth. (1 Tim 2:1–4)

Our moral crisis creates virtually all of our social ills including personal irresponsibility, sexual promiscuity, sexual perversion, family breakdowns, abortion-on-demand, neo-natal infanticide, marriage redefinition, illicit drug use, alcohol abuse, exploding crime rates, and more. A recent survey of culture and values in America conducted for the Culture and Media Institute reports that three-fourths of Americans are convinced that our moral values are weaker than they were twenty years ago. Nearly half (48 percent) even believe our values are *much* weaker.

A *USA Today* sponsored "American Religious Identification Survey" of adult Americans reports that 76 percent of Americans claim to be "Christian." Tragically though, according to the Barna Research Group, 53 per-

cent of conservative Christians even doubt there is "absolute truth." The
Barna survey may explain the surprising fact that so few professing
Christians believe in absolute truth for it notes that only 7 to 8 percent
of them have any biblical understanding. Thus, Christians themselves are
a part of our moral decline. As with Hosea of old, we must recognize that
"My people are destroyed for lack of knowledge" (Hos 4:6).

Our current moral declension is the most pressing problem facing our
culture and our nation. Moral decadence, left unchecked, will lead inevitably to social collapse. Though in the historical long run Christianity will
eventually grow to righteous dominance in the world,[1] Christians must
labor in the present to be a part of the solution to the contemporary
moral problem. And this means that we must renew our commitment to
Scripture by studying it more diligently, believing it more deeply,
applying it more fully, and defending it more vigorously. Our Lord Jesus
Christ prays for us just before dying to save us from our sin: "Sanctify
them in the truth; Thy word is truth" (John 17:17). He certainly does not
doubt the existence of absolute truth.

For our present purpose, we must understand that contained within
the absolute truth of God's Word we find his solution to man's moral
confusion: God's absolute standard for righteousness contained in his
holy Law.

> Your righteousness is an everlasting righteousness, / And Your law is
> truth. (Psa 119:142)
>
> The sum of Your word is truth, / And every one of Your righteous ordi-
> nances is everlasting. (Psa 119:160)
>
> The LORD was pleased for His righteousness' sake To make the law great and
> glorious. (Isa. 42:21)
>
> So then, then Law is holy, and the commandment is holy and righteous and
> good (Rom. 7:12).

Unfortunately, contemporary theological discussions too quickly
dismiss any consideration of both the *legitimacy* of God's Law in the new

---

[1] For a presentation and defense of Christianity's ultimate victory, see our
first Made *Easy* Series book: Kenneth L. Gentry, Jr., *Postmillennialism Made Easy* (2d.
ed.: Chesnee, S.C.: Victorious Hope, 2020). Keith A Mathison, *Postmillennialism:
An Eschatology of Hope* (Phillipsburg, N.J.: P & R, 1999). John Jefferson Davis, *Christ's
Victorious Kingdom: Postmillennialism Reconsidered* (Grand Rapids: Baker, 1986). For
a more detailed study see Gentry, *He Shall Have Dominion: A Postmillennial Eschatology* (Draper, Vir.: ApologeticsGroup Media, 2009).

covenant era and the *applicability* of it in the modern world setting. Generally this hasty dismissal arises from two pragmatic factors.

First, *promoting God's Law today requires too bold a commitment*. Promoting God's Law as the ethical standard for modern society issues a radical call to apply the *whole* of God's Word to the *whole* of life. This is out of step with both modern evangelicalism as well as historic fundamentalism. Evangelicals tend to be faddish (being drawn belatedly into the secular humanist cultural wake by attaching Bible verses to secular policies), dichotomistic (imposing sacred-secular distinctions upon social issues outside the sphere of the Church), and ambivalent (too prone to "reinterpret" the Scriptures when they run contrary to contemporary mores). Fundamentalists tend to be compartmentalists (as dispensationalists they so segment biblical revelation that God's Law becomes God's Word emeritus), myopic (their commitment to an any-moment coming of Christ theoretically forbids any long-range historical plans), and defeatist (their premillennialism views the Church Age as a time of inevitable failure rather than gradual conquest).

Proponents of God's Law call upon the Christian not only to consider the large-scale implications of the Christian faith for developing a Christian culture, but also to act upon that consideration from a distinctly *biblical* perspective. We promote an alternative way of seeing, thinking, deciding, and acting in the world — a way that differs from the dominant secular society all around us. As Reformed apologist Cornelius Van Til notes: "There is then not a square inch of space where, nor a minute of time when, the believer in Christ can withdraw from the responsibility of being a soldier of the cross. . . . Satan must be driven from the field and Christ must rule."[2] His disciple, Reformed theologian Greg L. Bahnsen, urges Christians to adopt a Christian world-and-life view "where all of our thinking and activity in every area of life is pursued in submission to the Lord Jesus Christ speaking in His word."[3]

To propose God's Law as an ethical option in the current context is written off as antiquarian ("that's the Old Testament!"), naive ("that will never work!"), and triumphalistic ("you assume Christianity will win the victory!"). Advocates of a rigorously Bible-based ethic demand deep bibli-

---

[2] Cornelius Van Til, *Christianity in Conflict* (Philadelphia: Westminster Theological Seminary, 1962–64, syllabus), 1:ii.

[3] Greg L. Bahnsen, *Van Til's Apologetic: Readings & Analysis* (Phillipsburg, N.J.: P and R, 1998), 20 n65.

cal study and committed Christian action. And they demand this in an age
of padded pews, air-conditioned "worship centers," and a tolerably com-
fortable social status quo.

Second, *promoting God's Law today is potentially embarrassing*. Since
defenders of God's Law issue a clarion call to Christian commitment in all
of life, those Christians who do not adopt such an ethic find themselves
to be "leftists" of sorts. By that I meant that when a position is to your
right, then you are to its left. This embarrasses both retreatist fundamentalists and status quo evangelicals who would prefer not to appear
to be on the left. As a consequence, advocates of God's Law are generally
ignored and the large cultural issues are simply not treated from a whole-
Bible perspective today.

The purpose of this small Made *Easy* Series book is briefly to intro-
duce the reader in a non-technical way to the case for the continuing
validity of God's Law in ethics — not only in the personal realm, but in
the social and legal spheres as well. Because of the oftentimes compli-
cated nature of the debate, many of those committed Christians who
might be sincerely interested in hearing the case presented from Scripture have felt at a loss for material to consider. I hope that this intro-
ductory study of the Christian theistic ethic rooted in God's revealed Law
might minister to those who have not been able to wade through the
larger and more academic works on the subject.[4]

A Proposed Position

Before I actually begin considering the applicability of God's Law
today, I need to state some basic distinctives of this ethical position. This
is important for clarifying what I believe the application of biblical Law
entails — as well as what it does *not* entail. Much confusion reigns over
ethics as a whole, and especially over the specific ethical commitment I
will be presenting.

Broadly speaking, an ethic rooted in God's Law holds that God's
express revelation in his written Word must be the ultimate standard by
which we determine right and wrong rather than any theory of "natural
law." "Natural law" theorists propose the existence of unwritten, universal moral principles that are determined by and therefore latent in

---

[4] Greg L. Bahnsen, *Theonomy in Christian Ethics* (3d. ed.: Nacogdoches, Tex.:
Covenant Media, 2002). R. J. Rushdoony, *The Institutes of Biblical Law* (Phillipsburg,
N.J.: P & R, 1973).

nature — including in man's own nature — and which are accessed through man's reasoning process. Of course, as Christians we hold that whatever natural law there might be must ultimately come from nature's Creator. Consequently, any natural law must *necessarily* be compatible with rather than contradictory to God's objective, self-revelation in Scripture.

More narrowly conceived, I will be demonstrating and defending the righteousness and practicality of even the Mosaic civil code for modern personal *and* socio-political application. This must necessarily become the position for the Christian who believes with Van Til that "it is this point particularly that makes it necessary for the Christian to maintain without apology and without concession that it *is Scripture, and Scripture alone*, in the light of which all moral questions must be answered."[5]

By way of introducing our topic I will summarily present six distinctives or qualifiers for this God's-law ethic, which must guide our investigation. Because of the nature of the debate and our special need for socio-political as well as personal norms, this book will focus specifically on the question of the *relevance* of the Old Testament Law today. Though Old Testament Law includes the Mosaic legal code it is actually wider, for it includes the full range of Old Testament revelation.

Let us now consider our six distinctives.

1. *God's Law is binding.* As God's creatures living in God's world, under God's dominion, and facing God's judgment, all men are obliged to obey God's Law. It is God's direct, propositional revelation which he has given to govern not only our personal actions but also our social and even political conduct. The Christian must see God's Law as a guide for his own personal *behavior*. God's Law is *law*, not suggestion. It is fundamentally obligatory, not merely recommended.

2. *God's Law is relevant.* In that God is all-wise, all-knowing, and all-powerful, all that he commands is practical for all times and applicable in all situations. God's revelation is not relevant simply within its own original time due to limitations in God's understanding. Van Til states that we must "seek the maintenance of God's laws for men everywhere and at all times, in ways that are themselves in accord with those laws."[6]

---

[5] Cornelius Van Til, *The Defense of the Faith* (3d. ed.: Phillipsburg, N.J.: P and R, 1967), 71.

[6] Cornelius Van Til, *Introduction to Systematic Theology* (Philadelphia: Westminster Theological Seminary, 1952), 245.

3. *God's Law is historical.* The Law is not a body of abstract, idealized principles dropped down to man from heaven. Rather it comes to us through God's supernatural inspiration of real men in history, and is designed to meet our historical needs. Thus, to properly apply his Law we must carefully interpret it by taking into account the full significance, purpose, and situation of the original intent of the various laws individually considered.

4. *God's Law is adaptable.* To properly apply it we must recognize the divinely ordained and revealed flow of redemptive history. That is, we must acknowledge the new precepts revealed in the New Testament and give them their full significance. Advocates of God's Law recognize that the New Testament is the conclusive revelation of God for man. If the New Testament repeals or annuls a particular element of the Law either by precept or by example that element is no longer binding in this era. But — and this is important — only *God speaking in Scripture* has the authority to do so.

5. *God's Law is multifaceted.* God's Law may be summarized in brief maxims, such as when God himself provides the Ten Commandments (Exo 20:1–17; Deut 5:6–21; cp. Exo 34:28; Deut 4:13; 10:4) as a summary of his fuller Law (Deut 4:13–14). Keil and Delitzsch call them "the kernel and essence of the law."[7] Christ also does this on an even more narrow scale in Matthew 7:12 and 22:40 when he teaches that the Law is epitomized in love.

Yet the Law's details remain significant and are essential in that they form the fundamental components of the Law, as parts to the whole. We may not render null and void the details of God's Law by preferring its generalized summaries. A forest requires trees. For instance, the love that epitomizes the Law has a specific character and content: it involves a behavior controlled by the moral strictures of the Law.

6. *God's Law is comprehensive.* God intends for his Law to be equitably observed by man on the personal, social, and civil levels of human existence. It is not designed purely for internal (spiritual), personal (private), or ecclesiastical (church) use, but for application in all of life. God himself is a social being (Father, Son, and Holy Spirit) and has created man in his image as a social creature (Gen 1:26–27). At the very beginning when he

---

[7] C. F. Keil and Franz Delitzsch, *The Pentateuch* in *Commentary on the Old Testament* (Edinburgh, T & T Clark, 1866-91; rep.: Peabody, Mass.: Hendrickson, 2001), 1:392. At Exo 20:1.

creates Adam, God declares: "It is not good for the man to be alone" (Gen 2:18a).[8]

7. *God's Law is behavioral.* By this I mean that God gives his Law to govern our behavior or conduct, including our way of thinking and planning. *It is not and never has been redemptive.* No amount of personal adherence to God's Law meritoriously secures our right standing with God, our personal salvation from sin, or our final entry into heaven. God's Law is redemptive only in Christ's keeping it in our behalf so that he and he alone might secure our salvation. Salvation is and always has been by grace through faith alone. Modern Judaism and Islam, along with liberal Christianity, are moralistic religions which promise salvation to those whose good deeds outweigh their bad. Biblical Christianity is a redemptive religion which promises to those who truly believe in Christ that they will be saved by his redemptive work alone.

These observations, in short, guide our approach to an ethic built upon God's Law. Our cultural moral condition is such that we need to get down to the basics before we can discuss specific moral questions. We need to ask what standard can secure proper moral judgments.[9] In *God's Law Made Easy* we will be considering the foundational issue facing us: the source of moral values, God's Law.

Let us now begin surveying the biblical argument for this approach to God's Law in the modern world. Since so many evangelicals deny its continuing validity, we must consider the Scriptural foundations for promoting God's Law today.

---

[8] See ch. 2 at "The Law's Purpose."

[9] Greg L. Bahnsen, *By This Standard: The Authority of God's Law Today* (2d. ed.: Atlanta: American Vision, 2015).

Chapter 2
THE ESSENCE OF GOD'S LAW

The Law's Nature
The Scripture defines the nature of God's Law in such a was as to suggest very strongly its continuing validity today. We may see this from a variety of angles.

The Law represents the presence of God
The written Law of God is unique in a fascinating way: it is the only portion of Scripture personally written by the finger of God. And Scripture repeatedly reminds Israel of this unusual action of God:

- When [God] had finished speaking with him upon Mount Sinai, He gave Moses the two tablets of the testimony, tablets of stone, written by the finger of God. (Exo 31:18; cf. 24:12)
- The tablets were God's work, and the writing was God's writing engraved on the tablets. (Exo 32:16)
- Now the Lord said to Moses, "Cut out for yourself two stone tablets like the former ones, and I will write on the tablets the words that were on the former tablets which you shattered." (Exo 34:1; cp. Deut 10:4)
- So He declared to you His covenant which He commanded you to perform, that is, the Ten Commandments; and He wrote them on two tablets of stone. (Deut 4:13)
- And the Lord gave me the two tablets of stone written by the finger of God; and on them were all the words which the Lord had spoken with you at the mountain from the midst of the fire on the day of the assembly. (Deut 9:10)

By this unique means of revelation God underscores the divine origin and holy character of his Law. *He himself inscribes it*. The New Testament employs similar language when referring to Christ's unique power over Satan which demonstrates the coming of God's kingdom in his ministry: "If I cast out demons by the finger of God, then the kingdom of God has come upon you" (Luke 11:20). Jesus states this to demonstrate that God's direct presence is experienced in his ministry (cp. John 1:14; 12:45; 14:9; Col 1:15; Heb 1:3).

Furthermore, God writes his Ten Commandments (the summary of and introduction to the whole Law; Exo 20:1–17; Deut. 5:6–21) on tables of stone to demonstrate their permanent significance. As John Calvin well observes: "the Law was registered upon stones, in order that the perpetuity of its doctrine should be maintained in all ages."[1] Keil and Delitzsch agree: "The choice of stone as the material for the tables, and the fact that the writing was engraved, were intended to indicate the imperishable duration of these words of God."[2] In that the Law represents the very presence of God, just as God is always present among men so is his Law.

The Law is the very heart of the new covenant

The new covenant is first recorded in Jeremiah 31:31–33. The New Testament highlights this passage in several places (Luke 22:20; 1 Cor. 11:25; 2 Cor. 3:6; Heb. 8:8, 13; 9:15; 12:24). The new covenant in Jeremiah 31:31–33 reads:

> "Behold, days are coming," declares the Lord, "when I will make a new covenant with the house of Israel and with the house of Judah, not like the covenant which I made with their fathers in the day I took them by the hand to bring them out of the land of Egypt, My covenant which they broke, although I was a husband to them," declares the Lord. "But this is the covenant which I will make with the house of Israel after those days," declares the Lord, "I will put My law within them, and on their heart I will write it; and I will be their God, and they shall be My people."

We must note that here God calls the Law given to Israel after leaving Egypt "*My* law." In fact, the law of Moses is repeatedly identified as the Law of Jehovah God, rather than merely the law of Moses. Note the following verses declaring this:

> Deuteronomy 30:10; Joshua 24:26; 2 Kings 10:31; 17:13; 21:8; 1 Chronicles 22:12; 2 Chronicles 6:16; 31:21; Ezra 7:6, 12, 14, 21; Nehemiah 8:8, 18; 9:3; 10:28, 29; Psalm 78:1; 81:4; 89:30; 119:34, 77, 92, 97, 109, 174; Isaiah 1:10; Jeremiah 6:19; 9:13; 16:11; 26:4; 31:33; 44:10; 22:26; Daniel 6:5; Hosea 4:6; 8:1; Luke 2:22–24, 39; 1 Corinthians 9:9

This new covenant is put into effect with Christ's establishing the Lord's Supper just before he is crucified: "And in the same way He took the cup after they had eaten, saying, 'This cup which is poured out for

---

[1] John Calvin, *Commentaries on the Four Last Books of Moses Arranged in the Form of a Harmony*, trans. Charles William Bingham, vol. 1 (Grand Rapids: Baker, rep. 1979), 3:328. At Exo 31:18.
[2] Keil and Delitzsch, *The Pentateuch*, 1:464. At Ex 31:18.

you is the new covenant in My blood'" (Luke 22:20).[3] We live today under the new covenant administration of redemption and are reminded of that every time we partake the Lord's Supper.

A major distinction between the old covenant and the new covenant is *not* that the ethical standards have changed. For Robertson notes in this regard that

> Jeremiah does not condemn the old covenant. He condemns Israel for breaking the covenant (Jer. 31:32; cf. Jer. 2:5, 13, 20, 32). . . . [He] indicates that as an integral part of the new covenant God will write his torah [law] on the hearts of his people (Jer. 31:33). The substance of covenant law will provide a basis for continuity between old and new covenants. Indeed, God shall write his will on the fleshly tablets of the heart, in contrast with the older engraving of his law on stone tablets. But it will be essentially the same law of God that will be the substance of this engraving.[4]

Thus, the problem in the old covenant was that the Law was written only on tables of stone, whereas in the new covenant it is written directly on the tables of the heart to ethically empower men. This, of course, alludes to the pouring out of God's Spirit to indwell his people so that we might better keep God's standards:

> For what the Law could not do, weak as it was through the flesh, God did: sending His own Son in the likeness of sinful flesh and as an offering for sin, He condemned sin in the flesh, so that the requirement of the Law might be fulfilled in us, who do not walk according to the flesh but according to the Spirit. (Rom 8:3–4)
>
> [God] also made us adequate as servants of a new covenant, not of the letter but of the Spirit; for the letter kills, but the Spirit gives life. (2 Cor 3:6)

The Law reflects God's character

When we survey the Scriptural statements regarding the fundamental character of God's Law, we quickly discover that the same moral attributes describing it also describe God's own character. We should not be surprised that the Law would reflect the Lawgiver's moral nature. And since God's own character does not change, neither should we expect his

---

[3] See also: Matt 26:28; Mark 14:24; 1 Cor 11:25; 2 Cor 3:5–6; Heb 8:6–13.

[4] O. Palmer Robertson, *The Christ of the Covenants* (Phillipsburg, N.J.: P & R, 1980), 281.

Law to change: "I, the Lord, do not change" (Mal 3:6a; cp. 1 Sam 15:29; Jms 1:17).

Let us consider a few significant moral parallels between God and his Law.

Goodness. On many occasions the Bible declares that God is good. I will cite just a few samples, then list several more addresses.

- Good and upright is the Lord. (Psa 25:8a)
- The Lord is good; / His lovingkindness is everlasting. (Psa 100:5)
- The Lord is good. (Nah 1:7a)
- And Jesus said to him, "Why do you call Me good? No one is good except God alone." (Mark 10:18)

Other references to God's goodness include: Psalm 34:8; 86:5; 106:1; 118:1, 29; 119:68; 135:3; 136:1.

Several biblical passages affirm the goodness of God's Law, reflecting the character of the one who gave it.

- Be careful to listen to all these words which I command you, in order that it may be well with you and your sons after you forever, for you will be doing what is good and right in the sight of the Lord your God. (Deut 12:28)
- Then You came down on Mount Sinai, / And spoke with them from heaven; / You gave them just ordinances and true laws, / Good statutes and commandments. (Neh 9:13)
- So then, the Law is holy, and the commandment is holy and righteous and good. (Rom 7:12)
- But we know that the Law is good, if one uses it lawfully. (1 Tim 1:8)

Other references also affirm the good character of God's Law: Deuteronomy 6:24; 10:13; Psalm 119:68; Romans 7:16.

Holiness. Not only is the second person of the Trinity called "Holy Spirit," but the Bible declares God to be holy scores of times. In fact, holiness seems to be his central, controlling attribute. Consider the following few samples.

- I am the Lord your God. Consecrate yourselves therefore, and be holy; for I am holy. (Lev 11:44; cp. 11:45; 19:2; 20:26; 21:8)
- There is no one holy like the Lord, / Indeed, there is no one besides You / Nor is there any rock like our God. (1 Sam 2:2)
- To You I will sing praises with the lyre, / O Holy One of Israel. (Psa 71:22b)
- And one called out to another and said, / "Holy, Holy, Holy, is the Lord of hosts, / The whole earth is full of His glory." (Isa 6:3)

- And the four living creatures, each one of them having six wings, are full of eyes around and within; and day and night they do not cease to say, "Holy, holy, holy, is the Lord God, the Almighty, who was and who is and who is to come." (Rev 4:8)

Other references to God's holiness include: 1 Samuel 6:20; Psalm 99:5, 9; Isaiah 29:19; 30:15; 41:14, 16; 43:14; 47:4; 54:5; 55:5; Ezekiel 39:7; Hosea 11:9; Habakkuk 1:12; Rev 6:10; 15:4.

Likewise the Scriptures often speak of God's Law (commandments, ordinances, statutes, judgments, etc.) as holy:

- In order that you may remember to do all My commandments, and be holy to your God. (Num 15:40)
- The Lord will establish you as a holy people to Himself, as He swore to you, if you will keep the commandments of the Lord your God, and walk in His ways. (Deut 28:9)
- So then, the Law is holy, and the commandment is holy and righteous and good. (Rom 7:12).

Righteousness. According to many passages God is righteous:

- Righteous and upright is He. (Deut 32:4d)
- So the princes of Israel and the king humbled themselves and said, "The Lord is righteous." (2 Chron 12:6)
- For the Lord is righteous; He loves righteousness; / The upright will behold His face. (Psa11:7)
- The Lord is righteous. (Lam 1:18a)
- In the future there is laid up for me the crown of righteousness, which the Lord, the righteous Judge, will award to me on that day; and not only to me, but also to all who have loved His appearing. (2 Tim 4:8)

Other references to God's righteousness include: Exodus 9:27; 12:6; Ezra 9:15; Psalm 7:9, 11; 116:5; 119:137; 129:4; 145:17; Isaiah 45:21; Jeremiah 12:1; Daniel 9:14; Zephaniah 3:5; Revelation 15:3.

Once again we may find many references to God's righteous laws, statutes, and so forth.

- Or what great nation is there that has statutes and judgments as righteous as this whole law which I am setting before you today? (Deut 4:8)
- The law of the Lord is perfect, restoring the soul; / The testimony of the Lord is sure, making wise the simple. (Psa 19:7)
- I will keep Your righteous ordinances. (Psa 119:106b)

- But now apart from the Law the righteousness of God has been
  manifested, being witnessed by the Law and the Prophets. (Rom
  3:21)

Other references to God's righteous law include: Psalm 19:9; 119:137,
160, 164; Isaiah 51:7; 58:2; Hosea 14:9; Romans 2:26; 8:4.

Other attributes. In addition we could note God's justness (Deut 32:4;
Psa 25:8, 10; Isa 45:21), which is reflected in his law (Prov 28:4, 5; Zech
7:9–12; Rom 7:12). And God's perfection (2 Sam 22:31; Psa 18:30; Matt
5:48), which characterizes his Law (Psa 1:25; 19:7; Jms 1:25). And even his
spirituality (John 4:24), which also describes his Law (Rom 7:14).

As servants of our God we may no more decry God's Law than we
may decry his character. His character is revealed in his Law; indeed, the
Law is a transcript of his character. We are to walk in the way he would
have us walk, in a way reflecting his own moral attributes: "Be holy, for
I am holy" (Lev 11:44, 45; 19:2; 20:7; 20:26; 1 Pet 1:16). "Therefore you
are to be perfect, as your heavenly Father is perfect" (Matt 5:48). Hence,
we affirm God's Law on the basis of its attributes.

The Law's Purpose
When we discern the biblically stated purposes of the Law, nothing
suggests that it should be inappropriate for our day. Indeed, its God-
ordained purpose commends it to the modern Christian — as well as to
all mankind.

Though we may present a great many purposes for God revealing his
Law, I will focus on six that are directly relevant for our consideration in
demonstrating its continuing validity. Having already summarized the
Law's very nature, once we take the next step in seeking to understand
its *purpose* the argument against God's Law should be over for those who
believe the Bible. Not only does the Law reflect the moral attributes of
God, but it also presents God's moral expectations for man.

The Law defines sin
Man's fundamental problem is ethical, rooted in his rebellion against
God; it is not ontological, caused by his being finite. This fact is vitally
important for understanding our relationship to God and our condition
and place in the world. Sin is the world's greatest problem, the root of all
other human problems (Rom 3:10, 23).

Genesis reveals the historical source of all our woes: Adam's fall in
Eden (Gen 3:1–8). But before this, when God creates Adam he commis-

sions him as the image of God to bring the entire world under his rule (Gen 1:26–27; Psa 8:3–9). Thus, the whole world is at Adam's disposal as God's appointed ruler over creation. But his rule is not without conditions. As a man he (and we!) is obliged to recognize that he is the creature and is subject to the Creator. Though he has a high and noble calling, it is subject to God's ultimate rule.

God presents Adam with an ethical test in the Garden of Eden. He sets apart one tree from all the rest, calling it "the tree of the knowledge of good and evil." In distinguishing this lone tree, God warns Adam that he must not "eat from it" (Gen 2:16–17; 3:11, 17). This is to test him to see if he would let God be God in determining good and evil (ethics). Or would he arrogate this divine prerogative to himself, attempting to be "like God"? When Satan approaches Eve in Eden he impugns God's character implying that God is arrogant: "God knows that in the day you eat from it your eyes will be opened, and you will be like God, knowing [determining] good and evil" (Gen 3:5, cp. v. 22). Adam and Eve evaluate the tree on their own and determine that God is wrong for prohibiting their partaking of it (Gen 3:6). Their partaking results in God's curse upon Adam and Eve, the whole human race, and the entire creation (Gen 3: 8–19) requiring man's banishment from Eden and his separation from God (Gen 3:23–24).

Because of Adam's fall, his sin pollutes the entire human race: "through one man sin entered into the world, and death through sin, and so death spread to all men, because all sinned" (Rom 5:12; cf vv 13–21; 1 Cor 5:21–22). From that moment the whole of creation "was subjected to futility" so that it "groans and suffers the pains of childbirth together until now" (Rom 8:20, 21). The universal prevalence and debilitating character of sin affects every aspect of man's being and all human endeavor, distorting all of reality: "Even though they knew God, they did not honor Him as God, or give thanks; but they became futile in their speculations, and their foolish heart was darkened" (Rom 1:21; cp. Eph 2:2; 4:17–20, 22).

We cannot understand our current situation apart from the intrusion of sin as an "unnatural" factor in God's originally good creation (Gen 1:31). So then, our fundamental problem is *ethical*, related to our moral rebellion against a perfect and holy God and his moral attributes. As such our rebellion breaks God's Law which reflects God's moral attributes "because the mind set on the flesh is hostile toward God; for it does not subject itself to the law of God, for it is not even able to do so; and those who are in the flesh cannot please God" (Rom 8:7–8).

Since our problem is primarily ethical, and since our sin blinds us to righteousness, God's Law is essential to our struggle against sin because the Law defines it. Indeed, "where there is no law, neither is there violation" (Rom 4:15). That is, without God's Law we cannot properly understand what sin is: how can there be an ethical violation if there is no ethical standard? Some sort of law is necessary as a criterion for distinguishing sin from righteousness. Adam chose the law of his own mind to determine right and wrong; but God himself is and must always be the ultimate standard of righteousness. God must define sin, and he does so in Scripture. And there we learn the significance of God's Law in this regard.

- Through the Law comes the knowledge of sin. (Rom 3:20b)
- For until the Law sin was in the world, but sin is not imputed when there is no law. (Rom 5:13)
- On the contrary, I would not have known sin except through the law. For I would not have known covetousness unless the law had said, You shall not covet. (Rom 7:7b)
- Whoever commits sin also commits lawlessness, and sin is transgression of the law. (1 John 3:4 KJV)

We must understand that the New Testament's many references to "lawlessness" (anomia, sometimes translated "iniquity") refer to breaches of God's Law.[5] For instance, consider the following samples. Jesus teaches his followers about Judgment Day, noting about false converts that "then I will declare to them, 'I never knew you; depart from Me, you who practice lawlessness'" (Matt 7:23). This obviously has *God's* revealed Law as its backdrop because:

(1) Jesus is speaking to a Jewish audience, who would naturally think in these terms. Note how the New Testament cites the Old Testament in this regard: "Blessed are those whose lawless deeds have been forgiven, / And whose sins have been covered" (Rom 4:7 citing Psa 32:1). The

---

[5] *Anomia* (and *anomos*) is a compound Greek word based on *a* (which is the negative, meaning "no") and *nomos* (which is the word for "law"). "Lawlessness/iniquity" is found in the following passages. *Anomia*: Matt 7:23; 13:41; 23:28; 24:12; Rom 4:7; 6:19; 2 Cor 6:14; 2 Thess 2:3, 7; Tit 2:14; Heb 1:9; 10:17; 1 John 3:4. *Anomos*: Luke 22:37; Acts 2:23; 1 Cor 9:21; 2 Thess 2:8; 1 Tim 1:9; 2 Pet 2:8. *Anomos*: Rom 2:12.

Hebrew poetic structure of Psalm 32:1 parallels "lawless deeds" with "sins." We see the same in Hebrews 10:17, which cites Jeremiah 31:34: "And their sins and their lawless deeds / I will remember no more." Again "sins" are "*lawless* deeds."

(2) In his first recorded major discourse, the Sermon on the Mount, Jesus expounds God's Law. And early on in that discourse he even states: "Do not think that I came to abolish the Law or the Prophets; I did not come to abolish" (Matt 5:17). We see how this is so in Matthew 5:21–28. He even summarizes the Law as the standard for our ethical treatment of others: "Therefore, however you want people to treat you, so treat them, for this is the Law and the Prophets" (Matt 7:12).

Paul uses the term "lawlessness" similarly in 1 Timothy 1:9. There he states: "law is not made for a righteous man, but for those who are lawless and rebellious." This not only relates the Law to "lawless" deeds, but clearly demonstrates that God's Law is what defines those deeds as "lawless."

In fact, in their writings both Paul and John not only speak of "lawlessness" but expressly mention God's Law, referring to it with high regard as supreme ethical authority. Paul speaks of God's Law in Romans 2:12–27; 3:19–31; 4:13–16; 5:13, 20; 7:4–9, 12–16; 8:4, 7; 13:8, 10. John refers to it in 1 John 2:3–4; 3:4, 23–24; 5:2–3. First John 2:3–4 is especially significant: "By this we know that we have come to know Him, if we keep His commandments. The one who says, 'I have come to know Him,' and does not keep His commandments, is a liar, and the truth is not in him." Consequently, we must understand their references to "lawlessness" in terms of that Law, not any general consensus among men.

Again, Hebrews refers to Jeremiah 31:34 which clearly has God's Law in mind, for Jeremiah mentions God's covenant made with Israel when they leave Egypt and receive the Mosaic Law (Jer 31:31–33). The writer of Hebrews cites Jeremiah 31:34 stating: "their sins and their lawless deeds / I will remember no more" (Heb 10:17). So not only does he draw from an Old Testament passage referring to God's Law, but he equates "sin" and "lawless deeds."

Clearly then, God's Law defines sin. And we should expect this — for it reflects God's moral attributes. God's moral character is our ultimate moral standard — as Adam learns the hard way.

The Law convicts of sin

Since the Law defines sin, preaching it convicts men of their sin. Preaching God's Law necessarily leads to conviction of sin in that the Law expressly prohibits sin, warns against its consequences, and judges it. Paul teaches that the Law is "spiritual" (Rom 7:14); Stephen refers to it as "living oracles" (Acts 7:38). Thus, like the Word of God itself (of which it is a part) the Law is "living and active and sharper than any two-edged sword, and piercing as far as the division of soul and spirit, of both joints and marrow, and able to judge the thoughts and intentions of the heart" (Heb 4:12). Consequently, as God's Word "it performs its work in you" (1 Thess 2:13).

Due to its pointing out sin, the Law actively stirs the heart regarding a knowledge of the death-dealing result of lawless behavior. In Psalm 119 the psalmist recognizes that shame comes from breaking the Law: "Oh that my ways may be established / To keep Your statutes! Then I shall not be ashamed / When I look upon all Your commandments" (Psa 119:5–6). The same is true in the New Testament as we see in the following verses.

- Now we know that whatever the Law says, it speaks to those who are under the Law, that every mouth may be closed, and all the world may become accountable to God. (Rom 3:19)
- What shall we say then? Is the law sin? Certainly not! On the contrary, I would not have known sin except through the law. For I would not have known covetousness unless the law had said, You shall not covet. . . . I was alive once without the law, but when the commandment came, sin revived and I died. . . . For sin, taking occasion by the commandment, deceived me, and by it killed me. (Rom 7:7, 9–11)
- Therefore did that which is good become a cause of death for me? May it never be! Rather it was sin, in order that it might be shown to be sin by effecting my death through that which is good, that through the commandment sin might become utterly sinful. (Rom 7:13)
- For as many as are of the works of the Law are under a curse; for it is written, "Cursed is everyone who does not abide by all things written in the book of the law, to perform them." (Gal 3:10)
- If you show partiality, you are committing sin and are convicted by the law as transgressors. (Jms 2:9)

Elsewhere Paul teaches that "the sting of death is sin, and the power of sin is the law" (1 Cor 15:56). Kistemaker explains Paul's statement:

What is the sting of death? Paul answers: sin. And what is the power of sin? Paul says: the law. So, what is the relation of sin, the law, and death? Sin is the cause of death, and *knowledge of sin comes through the*

law. In brief, the law has a causative function. It *brings to light sin committed against God*. It gives sin its power, that without the law is dead (Rom.
7:8). The law, which is good, arouses sinful passions (Rom. 7:5), and as
such empowers sin. The law convicts and condemns the sinner to
death."[6] Thiselton agrees, noting that the Law underlines "human culpa-
bility," which the law appears to intensify.[7]

Thus, the Law convicts men of their sin against God. God's Law is living and powerful to convict of sin and unrighteousness.

The Law condemns transgression

The Law does not just expose sin for what it is (by defining it); it does
not only convict of sin (by showing how it offends God). But it also carries
with it the penalty of its infraction (by threatening divine judgment).
Thus, the Law clearly shows the destructive consequences of lawless
conduct. This is an important function of the Law when God reveals it to
Moses:

> See, I am setting before you today a blessing and a curse: the blessing,
> if you listen to the commandments of the Lord your God, which I am
> commanding you today; and the curse, if you do not listen to the com-
> mandments of the Lord your God, but turn aside from the way which I
> am commanding you today, by following other gods which you have not
> known. (Deut 11:28)

Consequently, in the New Testament we read the following regarding
the Law's function as an actual source of condemnation for transgressions:

- The Law brings about wrath; for where there is no law there is no
  transgression. (Rom 4:15)
- This commandment, which was to result in life, proved to result in
  death for me. (Rom 7:10)
- For as many as are of the works of the Law are under the curse; for
  it is written, "Cursed is everyone who does not continue in all things
  which are written in the book of the Law, to do them." (Gal 3:10)
- For whoever shall keep the whole law, and yet stumble in one point,
  he is guilty of all. (Jms 2:10)

---

[6] Simon J. Kistemaker, *Exposition of the First Epistle to the Corinthians* (NTC)
(Grand Rapids: Baker, 1993), 586. Emph. mine.

[7] Anthony C. Thiselton, *The First Epistle to the Corinthians* (NIGTC) (Grand Rapids: Eerdmans, 2000), 1302.

The Law drives men to Christ

The Law severely judges sin, leaving men exposed to the wrath of God. And since it cannot save, it drives men to Christ. By removing all hope in self and by threatening the eternal wrath of God against sinners, the Law is the instrument by which the sinner is driven to Christ to secure his mercy.

God's Law causes Paul to look away from himself and to Christ for salvation: "Wretched man that I am! Who will set me free from the body of this death? Thanks be to God through Jesus Christ our Lord!" (Rom 7: 24–25a). He gives his testimony in this regard, noting that in his Pharisaic past he considered himself blameless in regard to the Law, but eventually turned to Christ for salvation:

> We are the true circumcision, who worship in the Spirit of God and glory in Christ Jesus and put no confidence in the flesh, although I myself might have confidence even in the flesh. If anyone else has a mind to put confidence in the flesh, I far more: circumcised the eighth day, of the nation of Israel, of the tribe of Benjamin, a Hebrew of Hebrews; as to the Law, a Pharisee; as to zeal, a persecutor of the church; as to the righteousness which is in the Law, found blameless. But whatever things were gain to me, those things I have counted as loss for the sake of Christ. More than that, I count all things to be loss in view of the surpassing value of knowing Christ Jesus my Lord, for whom I have suffered the loss of all things, and count them but rubbish in order that I may gain Christ, and may be found in Him, not having a righteousness of my own derived from the Law, but that which is through faith in Christ, the righteousness which comes from God on the basis of faith. (Phil 3:3–9)

Elsewhere he points out that "the law was our tutor to bring us to Christ, that we might be justified by faith"(Gal 3:24). Thus he declares: "knowing that a man is not justified by the works of the Law but through faith in Christ Jesus, even we have believed in Christ Jesus, that we may be justified by faith in Christ, and not by the works of the Law; since by the works of the Law shall no flesh be justified" (Gal 2:16). God's Law never offers the hope of self-merit for sinners to save themselves (Acts 13:39; Rom 3:28; Gal 3:11). No man can ever merit salvation by keeping the Law. In fact, it causes them to despair of their own righteousness so that they might seek the righteousness of another: Christ the Lord.

The Law guides sanctification

The Law does not have the power to sanctify; that is the Holy Spirit's ministry as he operates through the gospel. But the Law sets forth the

God-ordained *pattern of righteous behavior*. This provides an *objective standard* for the Spirit-filled Christian so that he might know what God expects of him. Sanctification is not guided or governed by warm feelings, cultural mores, or doing-the-best-I-can. It is guided by the moral character of God objectively revealed in his Word.

We see this in the Old Testament where the Law operates within Israel:

- And you shall keep My statutes and practice them; I am the Lord who sanctifies you. (Lev 20:8)
- The precepts of the Lord are right, rejoicing the heart; / The commandment of the Lord is pure, enlightening the eyes. (Psa 19:8)
- Your word is a lamp to my feet, / And a light to my path. (Psa 119: 105)
- For the commandment is a lamp, and the teaching is light; / And reproofs for discipline are the way of life. (Prov 6:23)

This objective standard for sanctification continues into the New Testament. And the Law's function in guiding our sanctification is actually *enhanced* by the fuller internal ministry of the Holy Spirit:

> For what the law could not do in that it was weak through the flesh, God did by sending His own Son in the likeness of sinful flesh, on account of sin: He condemned sin in the flesh, that the righteous requirement of the law might be fulfilled in us who do not walk according to the flesh but according to the Spirit. (Rom 8:3–4)

God promises this new power to keep his Law when he prophesies through Jeremiah the coming of the new covenant (which comes in the institution of the Lord's Supper; Luke 22:20; 1 Cor 11:25):

> "Behold, days are coming," declares the Lord, "when I will make a new covenant with the house of Israel and with the house of Judah, not like the covenant which I made with their fathers in the day I took them by the hand to bring them out of the land of Egypt, My covenant which they broke, although I was a husband to them," declares the Lord. "But this is the covenant which I will make with the house of Israel after those days," declares the Lord, "I will put My law within them, and on their heart I will write it; and I will be their God, and they shall be My people." (Jer 31:31–33)

The Law restrains evil

When the Law is properly understood and its threats heard and feared, it exercises a restraining power within the souls of sinners. This is the end result of true conviction of sin. Regarding the precepts and

commandments of the Lord God (Psa 19:8) the psalmist declares: "by
them Your servant is warned; / In keeping them there is great reward"
(Psa19: 11). We see this in several contexts:

- I delight to do Your will, O my God; / Your Law is within my heart. (Psa
  40:8)
- Blessed is the man whom You chasten, O Lord, / And whom you
  teach out of Your law. (Psa 94:12)
- Where there is no vision, the people are unrestrained, / But happy
  is he who keeps the law. (Prov 29:18)
- For as many as are of the works of the Law are under the curse; for
  it is written, "Cursed is everyone who does not continue in all things
  which are written in the book of the law, to do them." (Gal 3:10)

When Law is published and enforced in the public sphere, it reduces
criminal activity by threatening judicial sanctions. For instance, when
"thou shalt not kill" is backed up by the sanction: "He who strikes a man
so that he dies shall surely be put to death" (Exo 21:12) the cost of
murder becomes quite restrictive. We see this affirmed in the Old
Testament when judicial sanctions are levied: "And the rest will hear and
be afraid, and will never again do such an evil thing among you" (Deut
19:20). "Then all the men of his city shall stone him to death; so you shall
remove the evil from your midst, and all Israel shall hear of it and fear"
(Deut 21:21).

This is as God designed it to be. Paul speaks of this function of the
Law in the gospel context of the New Testament:

We know that the Law is good, if one uses it lawfully, realizing the fact
that law is not made for a righteous man, but for those who are lawless
and rebellious, for the ungodly and sinners, for the unholy and profane,
for those who kill their fathers or mothers, for murderers and immoral
men and homosexuals and kidnappers and liars and perjurers, and whatever else is contrary to sound teaching, according to the glorious gospel
of the blessed God, with which I have been entrusted. (1 Tim 1:8–11)

Promoting God's Law is an important means for restraining sin in
society. Habakkuk laments that "the law is ignored / And justice is never
upheld. / For the wicked surround the righteous; / Therefore, justice
comes out perverted" (Hab 1:4). Sinners unrestrained by the Law are
dangerous.

Conclusion
A careful study of both the Old and New Testaments show a unified
approach to God's Law. We do well to note the Bible's teaching on the

nature and purpose of the Law. Regarding its nature, the Law represents the very presence of God in the way it comes to us (Exo 31:18), it lies at the heart of God's redemptive new covenant (Jer 31:31–33), and reflects God's own moral character (Rom 7:12). Regarding its purpose, the Law defines sin objectively (Rom 3:20), convicts sinners effectively (Rom 3:19), condemns man's transgressions (Rom 4:15), drives men to Christ (Gal 2:16, restrains sin in man's behavior (1 Tim 1:8–11), and guides the believer's sanctification (Rom 8:3–4).

Clearly the general teaching of God's Word endorses the Law as our ultimate ethical standard. But we should also look to our Savior himself to see what he teaches regarding the Law of God. In the next chapter we shall consider "Christ and God's Law."

CHRIST AND GOD'S LAW

The central person in prophecy and gospel is the Lord Jesus Christ: "Jesus is the spirit of prophecy" (Rev 19:10). Of his encounter with the Emmaus Road disciples after his resurrection, we read: "beginning with Moses and with all the prophets, He explained to them the things concerning Himself in all the Scriptures" (Luke 24:27). In Acts Peter preaches:

> Moses said, "The Lord God shall raise up for you a prophet like me from your brethren; to Him you shall give heed in everything He says to you .... And likewise, all the prophets who have spoken, from Samuel and his successors onward, also announced these days." (Acts 3:22, 24)

Consequently, "as many as may be the promises of God, in Him they are yes" (2 Cor 1:20). As a result of this Jesus teaches "that many prophets and righteous men desired to see what you see, and did not see it; and to hear what you hear, and did not hear it" (Matt 13:17; cp. John 8:56).

Several lines of evidence show Jesus' affirming God's Law for his new covenant people. In no way does he undercut the validity of the Law when he comes. In fact, he affirms, explains, expands, and promotes it.

Christ Expressly Affirms the Law's Continuance

Jesus confirms God's Law most clearly and powerfully in his first major discourse, the Sermon on the Mount (Matt 5–7). Therein we read:

> Let your light shine before men in such a way that they may see your good works, and glorify your Father who is in heaven. Do not think that I came to abolish the Law or the Prophets; I did not come to abolish but to fulfill. For truly I say to you, until heaven and earth pass away, not the smallest letter or stroke shall pass from the Law until all is accomplished. Whoever then annuls one of the least of these commandments, and teaches others to do the same, shall be called least in the kingdom of heaven; but whoever keeps and teaches them, he shall be called great in the kingdom of heaven. (Matt 5:16–20)

In the following paragraphs I will give a brief, running commentary on exegetically significant points in this passage. I urge you to keep your Bible open for consultation as I make the these observations.[1]

Early in the Sermon, the Lord urges his followers to glorify God by doing good works: "Let your light shine before men in such a way that they may see your good works, and glorify your Father who is in heaven" (Matt 5:16). And then he *immediately* begins discussing God's Law. His very next words are: "Do not think that I came to abolish the Law or the Prophets; I did not come to abolish, but to fulfill" (Matt 5:17). By this close association he is linking "good works" to God's Law, just as we would expect based on our study in the previous chapter.

The statement "do not think" (Matt 5:17) is an ingressive aorist verb that means: "do not *begin* to think." As he opens his ministry he instructs his hearers that nothing he will say should make them even begin to suppose that he might be opposed to God's Law. He does not want to be misunderstood as he corrects distortions and abuses of the Law that have arisen in Israel. In this Sermon (and elsewhere) he is correcting the *abuse* of the Law, not rejecting the *use* of the Law.

Furthermore, when he says, "Do not think that I came to *abolish* the Law or the Prophets; I did not come to *abolish*, but to fulfill" (Matt 5:17), he uses the Greek word *kataluo* which means to "dismantle, abrogate, dispose of thoroughly."[2] This word is used in his prophecy of the Temple's stone-by-stone destruction: "Truly I say to you, not one stone here shall be left upon another, which will not be torn down [*katalutetai*]" (Matt 24:2; cp. Mark 13:2; Luke 21:6). This word also appears in 2 Corinthians 5:1 where it speaks of the dissolution of the physical body in death: "For we know that if the earthly tent which is our house is torn

---

[1] For an exhaustive study of this passage, see Greg L. Bahnsen, *Theonomy in Christian Ethics* (3d. ed.: Nacogdoches, Tex.: Covenant Media, 2002), ch. 2

[2] That he is applying this to either "the law or the prophets" indicates that "Matthew sees the Prophets in relation to their 'legal' contribution . . . ; only this makes sense of the use of *kataluein* ["to destroy"] with the Prophets." John Nolland, *The Gospel of Matthew* (NIGTC) (Grand Rapids: Eerdmans, 2005), 218. The prophets were God's lawyers, sent by God against sinful Israel to charge her with breaches of his Law, that is, to bring a legal "case" against her (Hos 4:1; 12:2; Mic 6:2). Hence, God warns that he will call heaven and earth to witness against Israel (Deut 4:26; 30:19).

down [*kataluthē*], we have a building from God, a house not made with hands, eternal in the heavens."

Rather than allowing his hearers even to begin to think this, he announces that he is seeking the opposite: "I did not come to abolish, *but to fulfill*" (Matt 5:17b). The conjunction "but" here is known as the strong adversative (Gk: *alla*). It provides sharp contrast, as in Matthew 10:34 which exactly parallels Matthew 5:17 in form and structure: "Do not think that I came to bring peace on earth. I did not come to bring peace but a sword." Notice the strong contrast between the idea of "peace" and that of a "sword"; they are exact opposites. Likewise in Matthew 5:17 Jesus contrasts the idea of *destroying* the Law with *fulfilling* it; the ideas are juxtaposed as *opposites*. As Nolland observes: "'Fulfill' must be taken in a manner that allows it to be an appropriate counterpart to 'annul.'"[3]

The word "fulfill" (*pleroō*, Matt 5:17b) which the Lord uses here cannot mean or even imply one of its common meanings: "to bring to a designed end" (BAGD 828). This is true even though sometimes the word does mean just that (see: Matt 1:21; 2:15, 17; Acts 3:18; 13:27). If this definition were employed here, though, it would teach us that Christ lived out the requirements of the Law so as to complete its purpose and do away with it. But it surely does not mean that or anything equivalent to it because he *contrasts* this word with "destroy." And if we interpret "fulfill" to mean "fulfill so as to bring to a designed end," it would effect the very thing Christ denies: the abrogation of the Law. "Fulfill" here, then, must mean something different from this possible meaning.

In this context, then, the term *pleroō* must be understood in terms of another of its definitions: "to make full, *fill (full)*" (BAGD 828 [1]). That is, it is used here to mean "to fill up to full measure." This would indicate restoring it to its true, God-intended meaning in opposition to Pharisaic distortions that have emptied it of that meaning. This would mesh well with all that we have studied regarding the Law to this point. In fact, Romans 3:31 (though using a different verb[4]) states: "Do we then make void the law through faith? Certainly not! On the contrary, we establish the law." He appears to be paralleling the sentiment of Christ's statement

---

[3] Nolland, *Matthew*, 218.

[4] Rom 3:31 employs the Greek verb *histemi*, which according to the standard lexicon of our day means: "reinforce validity of, uphold, maintain, validate." BAGD 482 (4).

here. Clearly then, according to Paul the New Testament *confirms* or *establishes* the Law rather than abolishes or removes it.

We find support for this interpretation just three verses later in Matthew 5:20: "For I say to you, that unless your righteousness exceeds [*perisseue . . . pleion*] the righteousness of the scribes and Pharisees, you will by no means enter the kingdom of heaven" (cp. Matt 15:3– 9; 23:23). Jesus' words emphasize this by bringing together two terms, *perisseue* ["full, abundant"] and *pleion* ["more"] which literally means "to be full more than." Thus, his disciples must fill up the Law *more than* the scribes and Pharisees — for they effectively empty it.

As the leading teachers in Israel, the Pharisees so redefine the Law by their own teaching that they virtually empty it of its true meaning. Consequently, Christ teaches that he comes to *restore*, to *fill back up* the Law to its original, divine intention, thereby rescuing it from the Pharisees who are emptying it of God's meaning. Nolland comments in this regard: "The fulfillment language represents a claim that Jesus' programmatic commitment, far from undercutting the role of the Law and the Prophets, is to enable God's people to live out the Law more effectively."[5]

But there is more! The word "for [*gar*]" (Matt 5:18) introduces an explanation of verse 17. That which follows (vv 18ff), then, will *justify* the preceding statement (v 17). Furthermore, here when Christ says "truly" (*amen*), he is emphasizing the importance of the following statement. The Lord often uses this word to draw his hearers' attention to an important observation he is about to make (e.g., Matt 5:26; 6:2, 5, 16; 8:10; 10:15). Thus, here he forthrightly declares: "For truly I say to you, until heaven and earth pass away, not the smallest letter or stroke shall pass away from the Law, until all is accomplished." He is here comparing the stability of the Law to that of the Universe (cp. Matt 24:35; Luke 16:17; cf. Eccl 1:4; Psa 104:5; 119:90). The Law cannot be disannulled until the material heavens and earth pass away, which will not occur until God himself dissolves the heavens (2 Pet 3:13).

Once again underscoring his teaching on the Law Jesus states: "not the smallest letter or stroke shall pass away from the Law, until all is accomplished" (Matt 5:18b). The phrase "smallest letter or stroke" refers to the smallest Hebrew letter (the *iota*, which looks like our letter "i") and the ornamental strokes on the letters (we might say: crossing the "t"

---

[5] Nolland, *Matthew*, 219.

and dotting the "i"). Christ is concerned to show that God's Law in its totality is being promoted by him. In the Greek he repeats the word "one" before "the smallest letter" and also before "stroke." This provides even stronger emphasis: "not even *one* of the smallest letters nor *one* of the smallest strokes on a letter. . . ."

When he says this will be so "until all is accomplished" (Matt 5:18) we may literally translate it: "until all things are accomplished." This statement parallels "until heaven and earth pass away." In other words, not the smallest letter or stroke of the law will pass away before history ends.

As if he needs more emphasis, Jesus backs up and reiterates what he has just stated: "Whoever then annuls one of the least of these commandments, and so teaches others, shall be called least in the kingdom of heaven; but whoever keeps and teaches them, he shall be called great in the kingdom of heaven" (Matt 5:19). The phrase "one of the least of these commandments" repeats the emphasis of the smallest aspects of the Law in order to show its binding significance. If the least things are so important, how much more the large aspects of the Law?

In fact, the one who "annuls one of the least of these commandments" contradicts Jesus' teaching in this regard and is considered "least in the kingdom of heaven" (Matt 5:19). This denunciation impacts that person's status in the very kingdom which Jesus comes to establish on earth in the first century.[6] John the Baptist (Christ's forerunner, Matt 11:10–11) comes on the scene preaching: "Repent, for the kingdom of heaven is at hand" (Matt 3:2). When Jesus begins his ministry not long after John opens his, he also preaches this message of the nearness of the kingdom and therefore also urges repentance: "Repent, for the kingdom of heaven is at hand" (Matt 4:17b).

He later commissions his disciples to preach the same (Matt 10:7). Jesus sees John as the last of the Old Testament prophets, the last of the old covenant representatives. Thus, those who follow Jesus begin entering the kingdom of heaven (the new covenant) which he is establishing (Matt 11:11–12). As Luke's version puts it: "The Law and the Prophets were proclaimed until John; since then the gospel of the kingdom of God is preached, and everyone is forcing his way into it" (Luke 16:16). Many

---

[6] For more information on Christ's establishing his kingdom in the first century, see: Kenneth L. Gentry, Jr., *Postmillennialism Made Easy* (2d. ed.: Chesnee, S.C.: Victorious Hope, 2009), 25–34.

of the Lord's parables deal with the kingdom of heaven (e.g., Matt 13; 18:23 19:12–23; 20:1–16; 22:1–14).

Following this strong statement of the Law's validity and its importance to his kingdom, Christ decries scribal distortions of the Law through adhering to the *oral interpretation* of tradition rather than the *faithful exposition* of Scripture (Matt 5:21–48). Though a cursory reading of his following comments might suggest Jesus is speaking against God's Law, this cannot be the case for several reasons:

(1) Christ would not contradict his own teaching. He has just vigorously asserted that he is not opposed to God's Law, that it would continue in effect until history ends, and that anyone who claims to follow him and annuls the least of the commandments will himself be deemed the least in his kingdom (Matt 5:17–20). Surely he would not boldly and massively contradict himself beginning in the very next sentence (Matt 5:21).

(2) Jesus would not contradict basic morality. Consider the first example in his list: "You have heard that the ancients were told, 'You shall not commit murder' and 'Whoever commits murder shall be liable to the court.' But I say to you. . . ." (Matt 5:21–22a). Surely Jesus is not repealing the law against murder.

(3) Jesus would not contradict biblical revelation. We should note that Christ is actually contrasting that which is "written" over against that which "the ancients were told," i.e., he is contrasting God's Word with rabbinic tradition. Note what he states elsewhere: "Why do you yourselves transgress *the commandment of God* for the sake of *your tradition?*'" (Matt 15:3b). When Jesus refers to God's Law in its true, undistorted sense, he declares: "It is written" (e.g., Matt 4:4, 6, 7, 10; 21:13; Mark 7:6; Luke 4:17ff; Luke 10:26; 20:17; 21:22; 22:37; John 8:17; 10:34; 15:25; etc.).

Christ Emphatically Teaches the Law's Relevance

When the Lord rebukes the Pharisees regarding the Law, he does not confront them for keeping the small obligations of the Law, but for their doing so *while overlooking the weightier matters of the Law*:

> Woe to you, scribes and Pharisees, hypocrites! For you tithe mint and dill and cummin, and have neglected the weightier provisions of the law: justice and mercy and faithfulness; but these are the things you should have done without neglecting the others. (Matt 23:23)

They constantly make void God's Law through their traditions: "You are experts at setting aside the commandment of God in order to keep your tradition" (Mark 7:9; cf. vv 1–13).

In the Sermon on the Mount itself he teaches that the Law is the Golden Rule of service to man. "Therefore, however you want people to treat you, so treat them, for this is the Law and the Prophets" (Matt 7:12). If you treat men according to the standards of God's Law you are treating them in a loving way.

He teaches that God's Law even defines love when he responds to the Jewish lawyer:

> "Teacher, which is the great commandment in the Law?" And He said to him, "'You shall love the Lord your God with all your heart, and with all your soul, and with all your mind.' This is the great and foremost commandment. The second is like it, 'You shall love your neighbor as yourself.' On these two commandments depend the whole Law and the Prophets." (Matt 22:36–40)

Love which excels even faith and hope (1 Cor 13:13) is not feeling or nondescript action. It is obedient action guided by the strictures of God's Law.

Christ Clearly Upholds the Law's Civil Function

Christ even upholds one of the laws most commonly misunderstood and employed today in arguing against the continuing relevance of God's Law in the civil sphere. He upholds the law calling for capital punishment for incorrigible criminality. Even the parents of a dangerous individual are expected to turn him over to civil authorities for capital punishment:

> And He answered and said to them, "And why do you yourselves transgress the commandment of God for the sake of your tradition? For God said, 'Honor your father and mother,' and, 'He who speaks evil of father or mother, let him be put to death.' But you say, 'Whoever shall say to his father or mother, "Anything of mine you might have been helped by has been given to God," he is not to honor his father or his mother.' And thus you invalidated the word of God for the sake of your tradition." (Matt 15:3–6)

This piece of capital punishment legislation is frequently brought forward in disgust to demonstrate the absurdity of the Law's modern application. But this law should never be derided by the Christian for several reasons: (1) In this very passage our Lord and Savior Jesus Christ defends the application of this law *and* rebukes the Pharisees for circumventing it. He complains that such people "invalidated the word of God," calling them "hypocrites" who merely "honor Me with their lips" (Matt 15:7). (2) In aligning these two laws from the Mosaic code Jesus specifically declares that they are God's Law. Note that he states: "For *God* said. . . ."

(3) This capital sanction is in fact actually found in the Bible, which we are called upon to believe, defend, and promote. To mock a command found in God's Word as absurd or reprehensible is simply not an option for the Christian. In fact, such a response reminds us of Adam and Eve's reaction to God's prohibition in Eden: God commands them not to eat (Gen 2:16–17); but they see that it was "good for food" — so they reject his command (Gen 3:1–6).

Contrary to popular opinion, this capital punishment legislation applies to a son that is: (1) old enough to be a threat to the community through criminal conduct and (2) mean enough to be turned over to the authorities by his own parents. An explanatory expansion of this law describes this son as "a glutton and a drunkard" who cannot be controlled by his parents (Deut 21:18–21). He is a curse to his parents and a menace to his community. This is not a ten year old who refuses to take out the garbage.

Christ Perfectly Keeps the Law's Obligations

The Scripture teaches that Christ comes to keep the Law: "Then I said, 'Behold, I come; / In the scroll of the book it is written of me; / I delight to do Thy will, O my God; / Thy Law is within my heart'" (Psa 40:7– 8). The writer of Hebrews applies this verse to him (Heb 10:5–7). He perfectly keeps God's Law in his own life: "I have kept My Father's commandments, and abide in His love" (John 15:10b). Due to the nature of sin as transgression of the Law (1 John 3:4) Christ is sinless *because* he keeps the Law: "Which of you convicts Me of sin?" (John 8:46).

This being the case, he is our perfect example to follow in Law-keeping: "The one who says, 'I have come to know Him,' and does not keep His commandments, is a liar, and the truth is not in him; but whoever keeps His word, in him the love of God has truly been perfected. By this we know that we are in Him: the one who says he abides in Him ought himself to walk in the same manner as He walked" (1 John 2:4-6). Following after Christ and keeping his commandments are synonymous according to John.

Christ Ultimately Saves Us by the Law

We are lost because of the broken Law; consequently the Lord died and thereby "canceled out the certificate of debt consisting of decrees against us and which was hostile to us; and He has taken it out of the way, having nailed it to the cross" (Col 2:14). Thus, he came "to redeem those who were under the Law, that we might receive the adoption as sons. And because you are sons, God has sent forth the Spirit of His Son into our hearts, crying, 'Abba! Father!'" (Gal 4:5).

In fact, his death eternally punctuates the need for and the validity of the Law. Consider this: the Law cannot be set aside, even to spare Christ: "He who did not spare His own Son, but delivered Him up for us all, how shall He not with Him also freely give us all things?" (Rom 8:32). This is necessary because "according to the Law, one may almost say, all things are cleansed with blood, and without shedding of blood there is no forgiveness" (Heb 9:22).

As Paul teaches the Christian, whether Jew or Gentile, faith confirms the Law's validity: "Do we then nullify the Law through faith? May it never be! On the contrary, we establish the Law" (Rom. 3:31). If the Law cannot be set aside to spare God's own Son, how may we surmise that it will be set aside to establish the new covenant era? It is the standard of God's righteousness, the breach of which brings condemnation and the necessity of redemption in Christ. The cross is, then, an eternal testimony to the righteousness and the continuing validity of God's Law.

Conclusion

In the preceding chapter we saw that the Law reflects God's eternal moral character and that it is renewed for God's people in the new covenant. In this chapter we have seen the integrity and continuing relevance of the Law in light of Christ and his teaching. In his first major discourse the Lord clearly declares that his ministry affirms the Law. He states that heaven and earth will pass away before any detail of the Law fails. And he warns that if any of his followers break the "least" of the Law's commandments they would be "least" in his kingdom (Matt 5:17–20).

Not only so but, in this chapter we have seen that he teaches the Law's relevance in controlling all social relations (Matt 7:12) and defining the character of true love (Matt 22:36–40). He even upholds the Law's civil function and denounces the Pharisees for setting that aside (Matt 15:1–7). Thus, we should not be surprised that he perfectly keeps the Law himself (John 15:10) and saves us from the curse of the broken Law by keeping it for us (Heb 9:22). Christian theology, rooted in Christ's teaching, must therefore affirm God's Law.

Chapter 4

THE NEW TESTAMENT AND GOD'S LAW

As we look more broadly into the New Testament we will see that all we have studied thus far is confirmed. The New Testament is built upon the Old Testament and is rooted in Christ who establishes the new covenant. I will highlight a few New Testament thoughts that affirm God's Law. Christians who deny the relevance of the Old Testament surely will not deny the relevance of the New! But this is precisely what they must do if they discount the Law of God in the Christian's life.

The New Testament Assumes the Law

By the very nature of the case, the integrity of Scripture assumes the continuance of God's Law. God's Word is a unity revealing to us a coherent revelation from God: "The Scripture cannot be broken" (John 10:35b). The word "broken" here is *lethenai* which is based on the verb *luo* which means "to loosen or break." Note that "the Scripture" is singular. And note further that Jesus expressly states that as a single unit it cannot be loosened apart or broken down. The Old Testament is the foundation for the New. The New Testament's structural unity depends on its Old Testament foundation.

Paul puts this matter forcefully: "All Scripture is inspired by God and profitable for teaching, for reproof, for correction, for training in righteousness; that the man of God may be adequate, equipped for every good work" (2 Tim 3:16–17). The Christian's manual for holy living is "*all* Scripture" — not "part" of Scripture. *All* Scripture is given that the Christian might be "adequate" and "equipped for *every* good work." It is not just the New Testament that is so given; it is the whole Bible, "all Scripture," including the Law.

Furthermore, since Moses reveals God's Law and Christ upholds it, we should expect that:

The New Testament Confirms the Law

The three leading Christian virtues are "faith, hope, love" (1 Cor 13: 13; cp. 1 Thess 1:3; 5:8). Of these three virtues faith is the simple, singular, God-ordained instrument of justification: "For by grace you have been saved through faith; and that not of yourselves, it is the gift of God; not as a result of works, that no one should boast" (Eph 2:8–9; cp. Rom 4:5; 5:11).

That God graciously provides salvation by grace through faith is often set against any endorsement of God's Law today. Christians tend to draw a Law/Grace distinction that prohibits any recourse to the Law. For example, popular books whose very titles have urged this distinction are M. R. DeHaan's *Law or Grace*, Alva J. McClain's *Law and Grace*, Grace Livingston Hill's *Not Under Law*, and John F. MacArthur's *The Salvation Controversy: Law or Grace?* One of Zondervan's leading "CounterPoints" debate books involves not two views on the matter, nor three, nor four, but *five*: *Five Views on Law and Gospel*. Such is the widespread nature of confusion over law and grace.

Yet Paul, the great apostle of the new covenant (2 Cor 3:6), informs us that faith actually confirms the Law: "Do we then nullify the Law through faith? May it never be! On the contrary, we establish the Law" (Rom 3:31). Here he directly asks the first-order question in the debate over the relevance of God's Law in the new covenant age: "Do we then nullify the Law through faith?" The Greek word translated "nullify" is *katargeo* which means either "to cause someth[ing] to lose its power or effectiveness, *invalidate, make powerless*" or "to cause someth[ing] to come to an end or to be no longer in existence, *abolish, wipe out, set aside*" (BAGD 525). Paul goes directly to the fundamental question.

Then he resolutely answers his own theoretical question: "May it never be!" The phrase "may it never be" in the Greek is *me genoito* which expresses the strongest form of negation. Paul is fond of using this phrase to deny any possibility whatsoever of a particular prospect occurring. For instance, he uses this phrase to deny the possibility of man's unbelief nullifying God's faithfulness (Rom 3:4), the prospect that God is unrighteous (Rom 3:6), and the suggestion that we may sin as a means of increasing grace (Rom 6:2).[1]

After denying the possibility of God's Law being nullified, he affirms the opposite: "on the contrary, we establish the Law." Here he uses the strong adversative particle *alla*, which is used to provide a forceful contrast between ideas. This word means "on the contrary, *but, yet, rather*" (BAGD 44). When it follows *me genoito* it starkly emphasizes a difference between two thoughts (BAGD 44). Thus, rather than nullifying the Law,

---

[1] See also: Rom 6:15; 7:7, 13; 9:14; 11:1, 11; 1 Cor 6:15; Gal 2:17; 6:14.

the Apostle of Faith declares: "we establish the Law." The word *histimi* means "to validate someth[ing] that is in force or in practice, *reinforce validity of, uphold, maintain, validate*" (BAGD 482). Paul knows of no contradiction between Law and Grace. Faith confirms the Law in Pauline thought. Indeed, elsewhere he asks: "Is the Law then contrary to the promises of God? May it never be!" (Gal 3:21a).

Paul is known in the New Testament as the apostle to both the Gentiles and the Jews (the uncircumcised; Rom 15:16; Gal 2:9; Eph 3:8; 1 Tim 2:7). Nevertheless, he upholds the "Jewish" Mosaic Law as an ethical standard for God's people. When he writes to the church at Rome he is speaking to a pervasively Gentile church (Rom 1:13; 15:12; 16:4). He informs the Roman Christians that "the law is holy, and the commandment holy and just and good" (Rom 7:12). And he does this even though early in his ministry he battles Judaizers (Acts 15:1–2; Gal 2:15–16; 3:1–5; 6:12–15). Thus, despite their abuses, he affirms Judaism's Law because it is God's Law (Rom 8:7; 1 Cor 9:9, 21).

New Testament Teachers Use the Law

Unlike the general tendency among modern evangelical Christians, teachers in the New Testament readily employ God's Law. In their ministries the Law is not taboo or an embarrassment of any sort.

New Testament sermons are based on the Law

Our Lord is not hesitant to base his teaching solidly on the Old Testament Scriptures, including the moral obligations of the Law. When asked a question on an issue, he responds by pointing the questioner to God's Law: "He said to him, 'What is written in the law? What is your reading of it?'" (Luke 10:26). We should recall Matthew 7:12 also: "Therefore, whatever you want men to do to you, do also to them, for this is the Law and the Prophets." And his teaching on love in Matthew 22:40: "On these two commandments depend the whole Law and the Prophets." In fact, he directly teaches that "it is easier for heaven and earth to pass away than for one stroke of a letter of the Law to fail" (Luke 16:17). See also Matthew 12:5; 19:4; Luke 10:26; 16:17, 29–30; and John 8:17.

In Acts 22:12 Luke evaluates Ananias on the basis of God's Law: "And a certain Ananias, a man who was devout by the standard of the Law, and well spoken of by all the Jews who lived there." In addition to what I noted above about Paul, he even declares that he himself believed "everything that is in accordance with the Law" (Acts 24:14).

John appeals to the general relevance of the Law in Revelation when he commends those who keep it: "The dragon was enraged with the woman, and went off to make war with the rest of her offspring, who keep *the commandments of God* and hold to the testimony of Jesus" (Rev 12:17). "Here is the perseverance of the saints who keep *the commandments of God* and their faith in Jesus" (Rev 14:12). We should observe that he aligns keeping "the commandments of God" with exercising "faith in Jesus."

James does the same as John when he writes: "If, however, you are fulfilling the royal law, according to the Scripture, 'You shall love your neighbor as yourself,' you are doing well" (Jms 2:8). Here he cites Leviticus 19:8, and just three verses later he challenges them to keep the Ten Commandments: "For He who said, 'Do not commit adultery,' also said, 'Do not commit murder.' Now if you do not commit adultery, but do commit murder, you have become a transgressor of the law" (Jms 2:11). He does this after declaring "whoever keeps the whole law and yet stumbles in one point, he has become guilty of all" (Jms 2:10).

The reader may find other relevant references throughout this book. But for now it is noteworthy that these New Testament figures *assume without argument* that God's Law applies in the context of the new covenant Church.

Old Testament case laws are cited as binding

In Mark 10 Christ includes a case law alongside a sampling from the Ten Commandments when he directs the rich young ruler to obedience: "You know the commandments, 'Do not murder, Do not commit adultery, Do not steal, Do not bear false witness, Do not defraud, Honor your father and mother'" (Mark 10:19). The command "do not defraud" derives from Deuteronomy 24:14. Thus, this case law is placed on par with the fundamental Law found in the Ten Commandments.

The apostles do not fear citing Old Testament case laws despite the abuses of Judaizers (cf. Acts 15; Gal 2). When defending himself while on trial before Israel's high priest we read: "Then Paul said to him, 'God is going to strike you, you whitewashed wall! And do you sit to try me according to the Law, and in violation of the Law order me to be struck?'" (Acts 23:3). Here he alludes to Leviticus 19:15 and Deuteronomy 25:2.

When writing to the Corinthians Paul cites Old Testament case laws For instance, in 1 Corinthians 9:8–9 he writes: "I am not speaking these things according to human judgment, am I? Or does not the Law also say these things? For it is written in the Law of Moses, 'You shall not muzzle the ox while he is threshing.' God is not concerned about oxen, is He?" Here Paul challenges the Corinthian Christians to behave in a particular manner on the following basis: "does not the Law also say these things?" Obviously his *assumption* is the continuing validity of God's Law. In addition, he cites a case law and applies it to the question of financially supporting a minister: "You shall not muzzle the ox while he is threshing" (Deut 25:4). He does this again in 1 Timothy 5:18.

In 2 Corinthians 6:14 Paul warns Christians to "not be bound together with unbelievers; for what partnership have righteousness and lawlessness, or what fellowship has light with darkness?" This alludes to and expands upon Deuteronomy 22:10: "You shall not plow with an ox and a donkey together."

By this line of evidence we learn that New Testament authorities — including Jesus himself — not only does not consider God's Law passé, but they even assume, apply, and assert it in their ministries. We should not deem the Mosaic legislation to be God's Law emeritus if the Lord and his apostles do not.

Christian Conduct is Based on the Law

God's Law does not exist merely as an abstract theory in Christian ethical thinking among academics. It necessarily impacts our daily, practical Christian living. This is true for those Christians who never really consider the question of formal obligation in ethics — and even for those who *object* to the very idea of employing God's Law in the new covenant era. Christians often suffer intellectual schizophrenia in allowing a disconnect between what they believe and what they do. This is especially problematic in our day of superficial churches, shallow preaching, and materialistic Christians.

We can see the practical implications of God's Law in two quick samples from the New Testament.

Love is defined by God's Law

I previously touched on how God's Law defines love when I was focusing on Christ's public ministry. Now I will return to this theme and expand on it in by applying it to the Christian's personal life.

Following the example of Christ, the apostles also define love in terms of the Law. This is significant in that love is the greatest of Christian virtues: "Now abide faith, hope, love, these three; but the greatest of these is love" (1 Cor 13:13). It is *the* obligation that defines the true disciple of Christ: "By this all men will know that you are My disciples, if you have love for one another" (John 13:35). "And this is His commandment, that we believe in the name of His Son Jesus Christ, and love one another, just as He commanded us" (1 Jn 3:23). In the final analysis God, who gave us his Law, is our supreme example for love: "Beloved, if God so loved us, we also ought to love one another" (1 Jn 4:11).

Again we must recall that Jesus forcefully teaches that God's moral standard encoded in his Law defines love:

> And He said to him, "You shall love the Lord your God with all your heart, and with all your soul, and with all your mind." This is the great and foremost commandment. The second is like it, "You shall love your neighbor as yourself." On these two commandments depend the whole Law and the Prophets. (Matt 22:37–40)

Note that he teaches that both love towards God and love towards our neighbor must be controlled by God's Law. And not only so, but this moral-based love actually summarizes God's Law in that it presents our fundamental duty towards both God and man. The command from the Law to love one's neighbor is cited six times in the Synoptic Gospels: (Matt 5:43; 19:19; 22:39; Mark 12:31, 33; Luke 10:27), thus showing its significance for Matthew, Mark, and Luke.

Paul agrees with Christ on this — as we would expect. He also presses the matter several times in his own ministry:

- Owe nothing to anyone except to love one another; for he who loves his neighbor has fulfilled the law. (Rom 13:8)
- Love does no harm to a neighbor; therefore love is the fulfillment of the law. (Rom 13:10)
- For the whole Law is fulfilled in one word, in the statement, "You shall love your neighbor as yourself." (Gal 5:14; cp. Gal 6:2)

James, the brother of our Lord, does the same, even calling love the "royal law": "If, however, you are fulfilling the royal law, according to the Scripture, 'You shall love your neighbor as yourself,' you are doing well" (Jms 2:8). By "royal law" he is emphasizing that God's Law is the law of the ultimate, sovereign king, God Almighty. Over against any human law or personal feelings we must recognize our obligation to love our neighbor — because it is the law from our King.

Significantly, in this passage James is chastising the recipients for their favoritism in the church. And without any hesitation he roots his scolding in the Law of God. In the following verses he even elaborates further on the Law, citing two of the Ten Commandments and noting that breaking one law breaches the whole law: "Whoever keeps the whole law and yet stumbles in one point, he has become guilty of all" (Jms 2:10). He warns that to break God's Law in this regard is to *diminish* the Law's authority and set oneself over the Law as its judge: "Do not speak against one another, brethren. He who speaks against a brother, or judges his brother, speaks against the law, and judges the law; but if you judge the law, you are not a doer of the law, but a judge of it" (Jms 4:11).

John follows this pattern of thought: "For this is the love of God, that we keep His commandments; and His commandments are not burdensome" (1 Jn 5:3). He sees no excuse in failing to keep God's Law because "His commandments are not burdensome." In his second epistle he reiterates this directive: "And this is love, that we walk according to His commandments. This is the commandment, just as you have heard from the beginning, that you should walk in it" (2 Jn 1:6).

John's recourse to God's Law is not only important in itself (as inspired Scripture), but especially in light of his broader, anti-Judaic conceptions. John records Jesus' strong challenge to his fellow Jews: "You are of your father the devil, and you want to do the desires of your father" (John 8:44; cp. Rev 2:9; 3:9). And this challenge appears in his Gospel which opens on a tragic note: "He came to His own, and those who were His own did not receive Him" (John 1:11). In fact, John repeatedly records material showing that the Jews actively strive to kill Christ (John 5:15, 18; 7:1; 10:31; 11:8, 54). Thus, even though John's Gospel challenges and denounces Israel, he does so while holding to and promoting Israel's Law.

God's commandments are important

As noted earlier, Jesus affirms God's Law to such a degree that he warns: "Whoever then annuls one of the least of these commandments, and so teaches others, shall be called least in the kingdom of heaven; but whoever keeps and teaches them, he shall be called great in the kingdom of heaven" (Matt 5:19). Thus, keeping God's commandments is required of anyone who seeks to obey Christ. A true Christian must neither annul God's Law in his own life nor teach others that rejecting the Law is acceptable.

Paul clearly teaches the importance of "keeping the commandments of God" when he writes: "Circumcision is nothing, and uncircumcision is nothing, but what matters is the keeping of the commandments of God" (1 Cor 7:19). And why should we not expect this? After all, he describes the Law as "holy and righteous and good" (Rom 7:12). Indeed, he writes that God's Law is "fulfilled in us, who do not walk according to the flesh, but according to the Spirit" (Rom 8:4). Consequently, living under the influence of the Holy Spirit in the new covenant age will involve living in obedience to God's Law.

John agrees with Paul: "By this we know that we have come to know Him, if we keep His commandments. The one who says, 'I have come to know Him,' and does not keep His commandments, is a liar, and the truth is not in him" (1 Jn 2:3–4). Law-keeping does not save anyone; but according to John (and Paul and Jesus!) law-keeping provides *evidence* that one truly knows Christ for "by this we know that we have come to know Him." This is important enough that he mentions this fact again later in his epistle: "This is the love of God, that we keep His commandments; and His commandments are not burdensome" (1 Jn 5:3). John informs us that we should keep God's commandments because this is pleasing to God: "we keep His commandments and do the things that are pleasing in His sight" (1 Jn 3:22).

Gospel Preaching Depends on the Law

Sin separates man from God, for "all have sinned and fall short of the glory of God" (Rom 3:23). In God's eyes we are "dead in . . . trespasses and sins" (Eph 2:1). Consequently, sin is our biggest problem, threatening eternal consequences in that "the wages of sin is [eternal] death" (Rom 6:23a). The leading purpose of Christ's coming into the world is to save us from our sins: "The Son of Man has come to seek and to save that which was lost" (Luke 19:10). "The Son of Man did not come to be served, but to serve, and to give His life a ransom for many" (Matt 20:28). Before God will favorably receive us we must repent of our sins and turn to him in Christ.

Therefore, in the Gospel record both John the Baptist (Mark 1:4; Luke 3:3) and Jesus (Luke 5:32; 15:7; 17:3) preach repentance from sin. Of John we read: "he came into all the district around the Jordan, preaching a baptism of repentance for the forgiveness of sins" (Luke 3:3). Jesus announces: "I have not come to call the righteous but sinners to repentance" (Luke 5:32)

After his resurrection Jesus appoints the apostles to take the Gospel to the nations, urging that "repentance for forgiveness of sins should be proclaimed in His name to all the nations, beginning from Jerusalem" (Luke 24:47). Peter is the first evangelist to preach after Christ's resurrection. At Pentecost he stands before the Jews in Jerusalem and urges them to *repent*: "Repent, and let each of you be baptized in the name of Jesus Christ for the forgiveness of your sins; and you shall receive the gift of the Holy Spirit" (Acts 2:38). Here he (quite naturally) links repentance to sin (cp. 1 Kgs 8:47; 2 Chron 6:37). He does the same later:

- Repent therefore and return, that your sins may be wiped away, in order that times of refreshing may come from the presence of the Lord. (Acts 3:19)
- He is the one whom God exalted to His right hand as a Prince and a Savior, to grant repentance to Israel, and forgiveness of sins. (Acts 5:31)

Paul is perhaps the Church's greatest evangelist and missionary. When he preaches in Athens he proclaims the gravity of man's condition and the ultimate consequences of it: "Therefore having overlooked the times of ignorance, God is now declaring to men that all everywhere should repent, because He has fixed a day in which He will judge the world in righteousness through a Man whom He has appointed, having furnished proof to all men by raising Him from the dead" (Acts 17:30–31). According to his own testimony he preaches "to both Jews and Greeks of repentance toward God and faith in our Lord Jesus Christ" (Acts 20:21; cp. Acts 26:20). He does this because true repentance leads to salvation (1 Cor 7:10; 2 Tim 2:25).

As we can see from the above examples, preaching repentance is designed to bring the sinner under conviction for sin so that he might turn from it. What has all of this to do with God's Law? Much in every way! In chapter two above I noted the Law's *purpose*: God's Law functions not only to *define* sin (Rom 3:20; 5:13; 7:7; 1 John 3:4) but also to *convict* of it (Rom 3:19; 7:7, 9–11, 13; Gal 3:10; Jms 2:10). Since true gospel proclamation urges repentance from sin, promoting the gospel requires preaching the Law. How else shall men know what sin is, understand its seriousness, and sense its repulsiveness?

James shows how this works when he links conviction of sin to God's Law: "If you show partiality, you are committing sin and are convicted by the law as transgressors. For whoever keeps the whole law and yet stumbles in one point, he has become guilty of all" (Jms 2:9–10).

In fact, Paul deals at length with God's Law when confronting Jews regarding their sin.

> But if you bear the name "Jew," and rely upon the Law, and boast in God, and know His will, and approve the things that are essential, being in-

structed out of the Law, and are confident that you yourself are a guide to the blind, a light to those who are in darkness, a corrector of the foolish, a teacher of the immature, having in the Law the embodiment of knowledge and of the truth, you, therefore, who teach another, do you not teach yourself? You who preach that one should not steal, do you steal? You who say that one should not commit adultery, do you commit adultery? You who abhor idols, do you rob temples? You who boast in the Law, through your breaking the Law, do you dishonor God? For 'the name of God is blasphemed among the Gentiles because of you,' just as it is written. (Rom 2:17–24)

Thus, when the Law is preached, the world is convicted. For "we know that whatever the Law says, it speaks to those who are under the Law, that every mouth may be closed, and all the world may become accountable to God" (Rom 3:19). Law-preaching "brings about wrath" (Rom 4:15) from which only the gospel can save: "I am not ashamed of the gospel, for it is the power of God for salvation" (Rom 1:16a). Indeed, "having now been justified by His blood, we shall be saved from the wrath of God through Him" (Rom 5:9). Paul defines the gospel in terms of salvation from sin:

> Now I make known to you, brethren, the gospel which I preached to you, which also you received, in which also you stand, by which also you are saved, if you hold fast the word which I preached to you, unless you believed in vain. For I delivered to you as of first importance what I also received, that Christ died for our sins according to the Scriptures. (1 Cor 15:1–3)

In all of this we see the necessity of the Law for the proper preaching of the gospel. The Scripture denies any Law/Grace dichotomy. The Law and the gospel are inextricably linked.

Judgment Day is Based on the Law

The Law is not limited in usefulness only in time and on earth. In fact, the Final Judgment beyond and above history will be based on God's Law. We see an allusion to this in Jesus' warning about false prophets who profess to serve him: "And then I will declare to them, I never knew you; depart from Me, you who practice lawlessness!" (Matt 7:23). Their banishment is due to their practicing "lawlessness," i.e., living against God's Law.

Paul deals with this matter in somewhat more detail in Romans 2. There he compares Jew and Gentile, noting that on Judgment Day ("the day", 2:16a) both will be judged by God's Law. The Jews will be judged on the basis of God's Law as written, the Gentile on the basis of the Law written in their hearts (their consciences as created in the image of God).

> For when Gentiles who do not have the Law do instinctively the things of the Law, these, not having the Law, are a law to themselves, in that they show the work of the Law written in their hearts, their conscience bearing witness, and their thoughts alternately accusing or else defending them, on the day when, according to my gospel, God will judge the secrets of men through Christ Jesus. (Rom 2:14–16)

From this we see the confirmation of two important issues. God's Law holds a universal prevalence among men: in the Jewish situation it is a written on tables of stone; in the Gentile situation it is written on the tables of the heart. Not only so but this universal Law will be the ultimate moral standard which God will employ on Judgment Day. That judgment will not weigh man's merit whereby men may be saved through self-effort (Gal 2:16; Jms 2:10). Rather it will determine the degree of punishment that the unsaved receive in hell; men will be judged on the basis of their deeds (Rev 20:12; cp. Luke 12:47–48). We should carefully note that all of this is "according to my gospel" (Rom 2:16).

Conclusion

In this chapter we have seen another series of angles by which we may understand the continuing relevance and binding authority of God's Law. And as with the evidence from Christ our Lord this material also arises from within the New Testament itself. God's Law is not just a concern for the Old Testament saints.

We see that the basic *assumption* of the New Testament is that God's Law continues as divine authority in that it is one element of his written revelation to man (2 Tim 3:16–17). We see that the New Testament expressly confirms the Law rather than rejects it (Rom 3:31). These two facts being so, we are not surprised to see New Testament teachers using the Law as authority in their teaching. Indeed, conduct in the new covenant is governed by God's Law. We learned that gospel preaching itself depends on it. And in the end God will use his Law as the standard of evaluation on Judgment Day.

Clearly then, the New Testament continues God's Law as revealed in the Mosaic revelation. But some New Testament passages seem to contradict this position. How shall we understand those passages? I turn to this in my next chapter on "Alleged Negative Passages."

Chapter 5
NEGATIVE PASSAGES AND GOD'S LAW

Introduction

Despite the strong case for the continuing, binding, authoritative relevance of God's Law in the new covenant era and on Judgment Day, some New Testament passages seem to contradict this approach to the Law. In that we want to promote a *whole-Bible ethic* we must carefully analyze these passages to determine their meaning and significance. I will review these negative passages in light of three factors: argumentative backdrop, historical backdrop, and theological backdrop.

1. Argumentative backdrop. In the preceding chapters we saw the strong biblical argument for the continuing validity of God's Law. I would especially remind the reader of two compelling passages. In Matthew 5:17 Jesus states: "Do not think that I came to abolish the Law or the Prophets; I did not come to abolish, but to fulfill." In Romans 3:31 Paul declares: "Do we then nullify the Law through faith? May it never be! On the contrary, we establish the Law." The evidence in these two passages — and many others — is too strong to dismiss out of hand. The Scripture is non-contradictory: "the Scripture cannot be broken" (John 10:35b). We must interpret apparent contradictions in the light of Scripture's integrity and infallibility. These two passages should be especially compelling since they represent the very teaching of the Lord Jesus Christ himself and his greatest apostle, Paul.

2. Historical backdrop. Much of the historical background of the New Testament is the struggle of Christianity with the Jews. This conflict especially focuses on Israel's racial pride, ritualistic worship, Messianic resistance, and Scriptural misinterpretation. As the Apostle to the Gentiles, Paul particularly emphasizes this: "Is He the God of the Jews only? Is He not also the God of the Gentiles? Yes, of the Gentiles also" (Rom 3:29; cp. Rom 2:17–20, 28–29; 4:16). Romans 10:3 is quite powerful in this direction: "For not knowing about God's righteousness, and seeking to establish their own, they did not subject themselves to the righteousness of God" (cp. Rom 9:31).

John's Gospel opens by noting regarding Christ's coming that "His own [the Jews] did not receive Him" (John 1:11[1]). Then John immediately rejects Jewish pride and confidence while opening salvation to all: "But as many as received Him, to them He gave the right to become children of God, even to those who believe in His name, who were born not of blood, nor of the will of the flesh, nor of the will of man, but of God" (John 1:12–13). Salvation is not rooted in blood-lines; therefore biological descent from Abraham does not insure salvation (contra Matt 3:9; Luke 3;8; John 8:39; cf. 2 Cor 11:18, 22).

The debate with the Jews regarding the question of mandatory circumcision and Jewish ritualism can be perceived as contra-God's Law — if not seen in its proper context. We are so far removed from the Jew/Christian debate today that we may overlook its impact in the early Church.

3. Theological backdrop. More pointedly, the historical background in other instances is clearly Jewish legalism: "knowing that a man is not justified by the works of the law but by faith in Jesus Christ, even we have believed in Christ Jesus, that we might be justified by faith in Christ and not by the works of the law; for by the works of the law no flesh shall be justified" (Gal 2:16).

The Book of Acts shows a keen interest in resolving this problem of ritual law *and its relationship to salvation.* Peter's ministering to Gentiles causes a controversy among the Jewish Christians because of their continuing racial pride (Acts 10:28, 34–37, 45). By God's grace the matter is finally resolved and the Gentiles are welcomed (Acts 11:1–2, 17–18). After vigorous, wide-ranging debate, the Jerusalem council rejects mandatory circumcision as promoted by certain Christians who were former Pharisees (Acts 15:1–5, 22). Here we see their clear assertion of ritualistic salvation: "And some men came down from Judea and began teaching the brethren, 'Unless you are circumcised according to the custom of Moses, you cannot be saved'" (Acts 15:1).

No proper understanding of God's Law can be legalistic. That is, no truly evangelical application of God's Law can allow Law-keeping as a basis for salvation. So now let us survey some of the controversial passages in question.

---

[1] This statement appears to allude to Exo 19:5: "you shall be my treasured possession out of all the peoples." Compare numerous similar statements: Deut 4:20; 7:6; 14:2; 26:18; Psa 135:4.

A Survey of Passages

Those passages that appear to negate the use of God's Law today tend to fall into four general classes:

Class 1:   Passages that renounce the Law as a means of justification.

Class 2:   Passages emphasizing the death-dealing nature of sin as it relates to the Law.

Class 3:   Passages pertaining to the transient ceremonial aspects of the Law.

Class 4:   Passages that are simply misinterpreted altogether.

I will survey several leading passages and show how they fall into one (or more!) of these categories. You will probably recognize many of these verses from your experience with the debate over God's Law. I will begin with texts from Paul's writings since they are generally the first that are brought to the table.

Romans 6:14

The most famous passage thought to stand against the new covenant use of God's Law is Romans 6:14 which reads:

> For sin shall not be master over you, for you are not under law, but under grace.

This is a Class 4 passage that many use as a slogan rather than interpreting it contextually. Let us several responses to the improper uses of this passage briefly.

First, Paul would not contradict himself. If Paul rejects the Law as morally binding in the new covenant era, then he contradicts himself in the *same* letter. Before this passage he declares: "Do we then nullify the Law through faith? May it never be! On the contrary, we establish the Law" (Rom 3:31), even noting that the Law makes "all the world . . . accountable to God" (Rom 3:19). Just a few verses after Romans 6:14 he affirms the Law as our standard of righteousness: "So then, the Law is holy, and the commandment is holy and righteous and good" (Rom 7:12). Surely Paul would not present so confused an approach to God's Law.

Second, Paul would not set God's Law against God's grace. If Paul is referring to God's revealed Law per se, then he sets it over against God's grace. When Paul says "you are not under law, but under grace" he uses the strong adversative *alla*. This emphasizes a pronounced contradiction between the state of being "under law" and being "under grace." But when we look in the Old Testament we discover that God gives his Law as an aspect of his grace. In fact, the opening words to the Ten Commandments (the summary of the entire Law) clearly highlight the gracious character of God's revealing his Law to Israel. "I am the Lord your God, who brought you out of the land of Egypt, out of the house of slavery" (Exo 20:2). Then immediately follow the Ten Commandments (Exo. 20: 3–17).

In Exodus God repeatedly emphasizes his grace to Israel. For instance: "You yourselves have seen what I did to the Egyptians, and how I bore you on eagles' wings, and brought you to Myself" (Exo 19:4). He declares his grace and compassion upon Israel even as they live under his Law: "I will be gracious to whom I will be gracious, and will show compassion on whom I will show compassion" (Exo 33:19b). When Moses returns to Sinai to receive the replacement for the tables of stone which he broke (Exo 34:1–5) God describes himself: "The Lord, the Lord God, compassionate and gracious, slow to anger, and abounding in lovingkindness and truth" (Exo 34:6). Even the Aaronic benediction proclaims God's grace to Israel: "The Lord make His face shine on you, / And be gracious to you" (Num 6:25). Thus, the psalmist prays: "Remove the false way from me, / And graciously grant me Your law" (Psa 119:29).

Before entering the Promised Land Moses reminds Israel to keep God's Law: "Therefore, you shall keep the commandment and the statutes and the judgments which I am commanding you today, to do them" (Deut 7:11). In that context he reminds Israel that they should keep God's Law because of his grace to them:

> The Lord did not set His love on you nor choose you because you were more in number than any of the peoples, for you were the fewest of all peoples, but because the Lord loved you and kept the oath which He swore to your forefathers, the Lord brought you out by a mighty hand, and redeemed you from the house of slavery, from the hand of Pharaoh king of Egypt. Know therefore that the Lord your God, He is God, the faithful God, who keeps His covenant and His lovingkindness to a thousandth generation with those who love Him and keep His commandments. (Deut 7:7–9)

Law and grace are not antithetical; Law comes in the context of grace. Paul is not contrasting God's Law to God's grace.

Actually, Romans 6:14 is not even referring to the Mosaic Law per se. Rather Paul is speaking of a law-principle when he states "you are not under law, but under grace." That is, he is denying the very idea that salvation can be earned by living according to some standard. We see this indicated in the NASB translation by their not capitalizing the word "law." Elsewhere Paul condemns law-keeping as a means of salvation.

> I do not nullify the grace of God; for if righteousness comes through the Law, then Christ died needlessly. (Gal 2:21)
> You have been severed from Christ, you who are seeking to be justified by law; you have fallen from grace. (Gal 5:4).

Romans 7:4

Romans 7:4 is a Class 2 passage that speaks of the death-dealing consequences of the Law. Here Paul writes:

> Therefore, my brethren, you also were made to die to the Law through the body of Christ, that you might be joined to another, to Him who was raised from the dead, that we might bear fruit for God.

To properly understand this verse, we must carefully note that Paul says the *believer* died — *not the Law*: "*you* also were made to die to the Law " (Rom 7:4a). A rather big difference separates these two concepts! The Law is not dead, *we* are. In the context Paul is arguing that since the Law requires perfection, if we attempt to keep it to merit God's favor by our own power, we will fail. We cannot succeed because we are dead ("in trespasses and sins," Eph 2:1; cp. Eph 2:5; Col 2:13). Thus, using the Law for this purpose results in it actually holding us back from God as we are overwhelmed by its righteous demands and our own sinful deadness.

Once again we must remember that one of the functions of God's Law is to condemn sin. Law *condemns* sin; it does not *enable* righteousness. In Romans 3:19 the Law shuts the mouth of every person, making them accountable to God and his judgment: "We know that whatever the Law says, it speaks to those who are under the Law, that *every mouth may be closed*, and all the *world may become accountable* to God." This is precisely what Paul is demonstrating in the very passage before us. He is arguing that the Law is not the problem, *we* are.

Paul also gives his own testimony regarding the death-dealing nature of the Law, even while defending its glory (Rom 7:12, 14):

> What shall we say then? Is the Law sin? May it never be! On the contrary, I would not have come to know sin except through the Law; for I would not have known about coveting if the Law had not said, "You shall not covet." But sin, taking opportunity through the commandment, pro-duced in me coveting of every kind; for apart from the Law sin is dead. And I was once alive apart from the Law; but when the commandment came, sin became alive, *and I died*. (Rom 7:7–9)

We must remember Paul's background from which he has been converted: "Although I myself might have confidence even in the flesh. If
anyone else has a mind to put confidence in the flesh, I far more: circumcised the eighth day, of the nation of Israel, of the tribe of Benjamin, a
Hebrew of Hebrews; as to the Law, a Pharisee" (Phil 3:4–5). Thus, Paul's
point (as a Jew, former Pharisee, and zealot for the Law) is that in Christ,
he dies to the Law *as a condemner*. Paul does *not* teach that we have died
to that which he says (in the same epistle!) faith establishes (Rom 3:31),
sanctification needs (Rom 7:12, 14), and the Holy Spirit prompts (Rom
8:3–4).

Romans 10:4

Romans 10:4 is a Class 1 passage wherein Paul is rebutting misguided
Jewish attempts to earn salvation through Law obedience. Here Paul
states:

> For Christ is the end of the law for righteousness to everyone who be-
> lieves.

Many see this as declaring the final end of God's Law with the coming of
Christ in the first century. They argue that the Law prevails in the Old
Testament but finally and permanently ceases with Christ's first-century
coming in the New Testament. This is surely mistaken in light of the
following considerations.

First, Paul's wider context forbids it. Once again (as we see elsewhere
even in Romans) rather than dismissing the Law Paul actually affirms and
extolls it (e.g., see discussions of Rom 3:19, 31; 7;12, 14 above). To adopt
the view that he is here declaring the Law's cessation contradicts those
earlier statements of confirmation.

Second, Paul's immediate context counters it. Paul is, in fact, referring to the Mosaic Law for: (1) He is speaking of the Jews: "Brethren, my
heart's desire and my prayer to God for them is for their salvation" (Rom
10:1; cp. 9:30–31). (2) The very next verse expressly mentions Moses: "For
Moses writes that the man who practices the righteousness which is
based on law shall live by that righteousness" (Rom 10:5). But he refers
to the Mosaic Law in confronting and rebutting the Jewish tendency to
legalism. Morris well notes in this regard:

> Here Paul is saying rather that Christ is the end to the law as a way of
> attaining righteousness. This does not mean the abolishing of the law,
> for Paul claims that he is establishing it (3:31), and he claims value for it
> (e.g., 7:7). What Paul is emphasizing is the decisive end to all such claims

as those of the Jews (cf. 6:14; 7:4, 6; Eph. 2:15). The saving work of Christ has brought to a close any attempt to attain righteousness by way of law.[2]

This does not mean that salvation is secured in the old covenant by Law-keeping. for this has never been true. Rather it means that Israel *abuses* God's Law in *attempting* to use it for that purpose. Actually Paul goes on to prove that salvation by grace through faith prevails even in the Old Testament. He does this by citing Moses and Isaiah as evidence. After specifically mentioning Moses (Rom 10:5) he quotes from Deuteronomy 30:12 (Rom 10:6–7) and Deuteronomy 30:14 (Rom 10:8) then concludes on the basis of these verses: "if you confess with your mouth Jesus as Lord, and believe in your heart that God raised Him from the dead, you shall be saved" (Rom 10:9). He continues further by citing Isaiah 28:16: "For the Scripture says, 'Whoever believes in Him will not be disappointed'" (Rom 10:11). Paul's point is that God's people have never been saved by legal obedience, just as Moses and Isaiah prove. He is not declaring the end of the Law.

1 Corinthians 9:20b

In 1 Corinthians 9:20b Paul seems to disavow God's Law altogether, when he claims he himself was "to those who are under the Law, as under the Law, *though not being myself under the Law.*" How shall we understand this statement? Does Paul here renounce the Law as an obligation upon the Christian?

In this passage Paul denies he is obliged to "the Law" — however, he is referring to the ceremonial aspects of the Law, not the Law as a system of ethical obligations. This is evident for the following reasons:

First, the broader context points in a different direction. The broader setting deals with the debate Paul is engaged in regarding Jewish sensitivities — that is, the problem of eating meat offered to idols (1 Cor 8—10). The Jewish question forms the backdrop to the whole context. The focus of the debate over foods is narrowly Jewish.

Eating such tainted meat before a Jew or Jewish-Christian causes needless, offense. This would pose no problem for the Gentile Christian, as is evident from the Jerusalem council. The council merely urges Gentiles graciously (not legalistically) to forgo meat offered to idols solely for the sake of the Jewish Christians:

---

[2] Leon Morris, *The Epistle to the Romans* (Grand Rapids: Eerdmans, 1988), 381.

> Therefore it is my judgment that we do not trouble those who are
> turning to God from among the Gentiles, but that we write to them that
> they abstain from things contaminated by idols and from fornication and
> from what is strangled and from blood. For Moses from ancient genera-
> tions has in every city those who preach him, since he is read in the
> synagogues every Sabbath. (Acts 15:19–21)

Avoiding unnecessary offense is an obvious concern for Paul (Rom 14:13).

Paul concludes this whole three chapter debate declaring: "Whether,
then, you eat or drink or whatever you do, do all to the glory of God.
Give no offense either to Jews or to Greeks or to the church of God"
(1 Cor 10:31–32).

If the larger context has as its basic concern narrowly Jewish sensitivities and the controversy arising from that, then Paul's denying his
obligation to "the Law" would surely mean only the ceremonial law. New
Testament scholars recognize the "problem" of Paul's use of "the Law":
sometimes it means the whole Law; sometimes the ceremonial Law;
sometimes a principle of legalism. Only context can clarify which meaning
Paul has in mind.

Second, the immediate context focuses on cultural distinctions. The
setting of Paul's statement suggests he is dealing with "the Law" as that
which culturally separates the Jewish race from the Gentiles. In the very
verse in question Paul states: "to the Jews I become as a Jew." This idea
of "becoming a Jew" indicates ceremonial distinctives are in view rather
than moral ones. No one "becomes a Jew" by not killing, not committing
adultery, or not coveting (keeping the moral aspects of the Law). They do
"become a Jew" by undergoing the ceremonial distinctives which marked
the Jews off from the Gentiles (circumcision, food laws, cleansing rituals,
and so forth). For instance, if a non-Jew wants to partake the Passover, he
must be circumcised first so that he will become a Jew: "But if a stranger
sojourns with you, and celebrates the Passover to the Lord, let all his
males be circumcised, and then let him come near to celebrate it; and he
shall be like a native of the land" (Exo 12:48).

On one occasion Paul has Timothy circumcised so that they might
associate with the ceremonially-observant Jews in order to preach the
gospel to them: "And he came also to Derbe and to Lystra. And behold,
a certain disciple was there, named Timothy, the son of a Jewish woman
who was a believer, but his father was a Greek . . . . Paul wanted this man
to go with him; and he took him and circumcised him because of the Jews

who were in those parts, for they all knew that his father was a Greek" (Acts 16:1, 3).

Paul sometimes demonstrates his Jewishness by referring to his (past) ceremonial observance:

- I am a Jew, born in Tarsus of Cilicia, but brought up in this city, educated under Gamaliel, strictly according to the law of our fathers, being zealous for God, just as you all are today. (Acts 22:3)
- They have known about me for a long time previously, if they are willing to testify, that I lived as a Pharisee according to the strictest sect of our religion. (Acts 26:5)
- Circumcised the eighth day, of the nation of Israel, of the tribe of Benjamin, a Hebrew of Hebrews; as to the Law, a Pharisee. (Phil 3:5)

In fact, Paul can distinguish the Law from the ceremonial aspects of the Law — and he does so in 1 Corinthians. He distinguishes "the commandments of God" from circumcision (even though that is, in fact, a commandment of God): "Circumcision is nothing, and uncircumcision is nothing, but what matters is the keeping of the commandments of God" (1 Cor 7:19).

Thus, it seems this is further evidence that "the Law" in this verse refers to the ceremonial features of the Law.

Third, Paul would not undermine his broader practice. Although here in 1 Corinthians 9:20 Paul seems to deny the Law, elsewhere he vigorously affirms it as we have seen in our study. This would indicate he must have different conceptions of "the Law" in mind, which would fit the well-known distinction between the ceremonial and the moral aspects of the Law.

He affirms the Law as an ongoing obligation among those of faith: "Do we then nullify the Law through faith? May it never be! On the contrary, we establish the Law" (Rom 3:31). Surely "the Law" established in Romans 3 is not the Law dis-established in 1 Corinthians 9. The moral elements of the Law are expressly affirmed in Romans 7:12: "The Law is holy, and the commandment is holy and righteous and good." How could he disavow his obligation to that which is "holy, righteous, and good"?

Even the judicial elements and function of the Law are endorsed by the Apostle to the Gentiles:

But we know that the Law is good, if one uses it lawfully, realizing the fact that law is not made for a righteous man, but for those who are lawless and rebellious, for the ungodly and sinners, for the unholy and profane, for those who kill their fathers or mothers, for murderers and immoral men and homosexuals and kidnappers and liars and perjurers, and whatever else is contrary to sound teaching, according to the glorious gospel of the blessed God, with which I have been entrusted. (1 Tim 1:8–11)

Fourth, the historical issue revolves around the ceremonial law. The New Testament controversy between Jew and Gentile (which forms the backdrop of the 1 Corinthians 8—10 passage) invariably revolves around the ceremonial law. Thus, the ceremonial law causes the conflict, not the moral or judicial law. As whole books of testimony to this, we may consult both Galatians and Hebrews. Numerous references elsewhere distinguish the Jew and Gentile on the basis of ceremonial principles:

- "And he said to them, 'You yourselves know how unlawful it is for a man who is a Jew to associate with a foreigner or to visit him; and yet God has shown me that I should not call any man unholy or unclean'" (Acts 10:28). This passages clearly speaks to the food laws, as Peter vision of the sheet with unclean foods indicates.
- "And all the circumcised believers who had come with Peter were amazed, because the gift of the Holy Spirit had been poured out upon the Gentiles also" (Acts 10:45). Note the surprise of those "circumcised" regarding God's blessing on those uncircumcised.
- "And when Peter came up to Jerusalem, those who were circumcised took issue with him, saying, 'You went to uncircumcised men and ate with them'" (Acts 11:2–3). Note the angry resistance to Peter by Jewish Christians, because Peter associated with ceremonially unclean (uncircumcised) men.
- "And some men came down from Judea and began teaching the brethren, 'Unless you are circumcised according to the custom of Moses, you cannot be saved'" (Acts 15:1; cp. v. 5). Note the first major controversy between Jew and Gentile within developing Christianity is over the ceremonial matter of circumcision.
- "They have been told about you, that you are teaching all the Jews who are among the Gentiles to forsake Moses, telling them not to circumcise their children nor to walk according to the customs" (Acts 21:21). Note that "forsaking Moses" (the Lawgiver) is associated with not performing ceremonial rituals (e.g., circumcision).
- "And will not he who is physically uncircumcised, if he keeps the Law, will he not judge you who though having the letter of the Law and circumcision are a transgressor of the Law? For he is not a Jew who is one outwardly; neither is circumcision that which is outward in the flesh. Then what advantage has the Jew? Or what is the benefit of circumcision?" (Rom 2:27—3:1). Note that Paul discounts the value of ceremonial circumcision over against "keeping the Law" in its moral strictures.

Clearly, then, Paul's denying his obligation to "the Law," is a disavowal of *ceremonial features of the Law*. All of those have been fulfilled in Christ. For instance, Paul says we are "circumcised" when we are baptized (Col 2:11–12; cp. Rom 2:29; Phil 3:2). We become priests when we proclaim God's word and worship as Christians (Rom 15:16; 1 Pet 2:5, 9). We function as God's temple when we are converted and indwelt by God's Spirit (Eph 2:21; 1 Cor 3:16; 2 Cor 6:16).

2 Corinthians 3

Second Corinthians 3 is a mixed Class 1 and 2 passage. It presents the Law in its death-dealing sense over against those who attempt to use it for personal merit before God:

> Not that we are adequate in ourselves to consider anything as coming from ourselves, but our adequacy is from God, who also made us adequate as servants of a new covenant, not of the letter, but of the Spirit; for the letter kills, but the Spirit gives life. But if the ministry of death, in letters engraved on stones, came with glory, so that the sons of Israel could not look intently at the face of Moses because of the glory of his face, fading as it was, how shall the ministry of the Spirit fail to be even more with glory? For if the ministry of condemnation has glory, much more does the ministry of righteousness abound in glory. For indeed what had glory, in this case has no glory on account of the glory that surpasses it. For if that which fades away was with glory, much more that which remains is in glory. (2 Cor 3:5–11)

On a surface-level reading this passage does sound derogatory toward the Law: Paul presents himself as a servant of the "new covenant" (2 Cor 3:6a), contrasts the letter of the Law with God's Spirit (2 Cor 3:6b), warns that the letter kills (2 Cor 3:6c) and is a ministry of death (2 Cor 3:7a) and condemnation (2 Cor 3:9a), and even notes the fading of the Law's glory (2 Cor 3:7c, 11). But again we must allow Paul to be consistent with himself—and Romans affirms the Law over and over again (see previous discussions). What is Paul teaching here?

To properly understand Paul's point we must recognize the historical setting of the Corinthian church. When Paul initially visits Corinth he reasons with his ethnic brothers in the synagogue (Acts 18:4) by "solemnly testifying to the Jews that Jesus was the Christ" (Acts 18:5). Unfortunately, when the Jews "resisted and blasphemed, he shook out his garments and said to them, 'Your blood be upon your own heads!'" (Acts 18:6).

Nevertheless, Paul leads "Crispus, the leader of the synagogue" to Christ — along with his household and many others (Acts 18:8). This re-ignites the fury of the Jews, causing them to drag Paul before Gallio the proconsul where they complain that Paul "persuades men to worship God contrary to the law" (Acts 18:12–13). So then, the church is born in the context of the Jewish synagogue, involved the conversion of some Jews, and generates a dispute with the Jews over the proper worship of God.

Later in his first letter to the Corinthians Paul mentions his continu-ing effort to reach the Jews (1 Cor 9:20). And in 2 Corinthians he responds to the false apostles (2 Cor 11:13; cp. v 26) who are Jews that are proud of their Abrahamic descent (2 Cor 11:18, 22). Thus, the Corinthian church has a strong Hebrew element within it which causes friction and confu-sion.

So then, in 2 Corinthians 3 Paul is extolling the glory of the new cove-nant over against the common Jewish use of God's Law, such as that which is held by the Jewish false apostles. He warns the Judaizing legal-ists that the Law in and of itself brings death when such men attempt to use it (2 Cor 3:7, 9). He contrasts the Law's inscription on tables of stone with the Spirit's operation on the heart within (2 Cor 3:3) noting that the Spirit "gives life" (2 Cor 3:6). Paul speaks similarly in Romans:

> For what the Law could not do, weak as it was through the flesh, God did: sending His own Son in the likeness of sinful flesh and as an offering for sin, He condemned sin in the flesh, in order that the requirement of the Law might be fulfilled in us, who do not walk according to the flesh, but according to the Spirit. (Rom 8:3–4)

This is precisely the promise of the new covenant which both Isaiah and Ezekiel prophesy:

> "But this is the covenant which I will make with the house of Israel after those days," declares the Lord, "I will put My law within them, and on their heart I will write it; and I will be their God, and they shall be My people." (Jer 31:33)
> "I will put My Spirit within you and cause you to walk in My statutes, and you will be careful to observe My ordinances." (Eze 36:27)

Neither Paul, Isaiah, nor Ezekiel dismiss the Law; rather they see the Spirit as prompting Law obedience from within.

Galatians

In Galatians we have a large-scale argument regarding the Law which falls into two categories: legalism (Class 1) and ceremonialism (Class 3). The Judaizers were in Galatia urging men that they must keep all aspects of the Law *in order to be saved*, especially the ceremonial laws. Galatians is one of the earliest writings of the New Testament and was written near the time of the Jerusalem council in Acts 15. There we read of the problem the apostles and elders faces: "And some men came down from Judea and began teaching the brethren, 'Unless you are circumcised according to the custom of Moses, you cannot be saved'" (Acts 15:1).

Paul roundly rebukes such thinking. He argues that our hope for righteousness comes by the Spirit through faith rather than through the ceremonial strictures of the Law:

> It was for freedom that Christ set us free; therefore keep standing firm and do not be subject again to a yoke of slavery. Behold I, Paul, say to you that if you receive circumcision, Christ will be of no benefit to you. And I testify again to every man who receives circumcision, that he is under obligation to keep the whole Law. You have been severed from Christ, you who are seeking to be justified by law; you have fallen from grace. For we through the Spirit, by faith, are waiting for the hope of righteousness. (Gal 5:1–5)

Furthermore, he teaches that Christ alone delivers us from the curse of the broken Law: "Christ redeemed us from the curse of the Law, having become a curse for us — for it is written, 'Cursed is everyone who hangs on a tree'" (Gal 3:13). The Law itself is not a "curse," but it *contains* a curse — *for those who break it.* Thus, "a man is not justified by the works of the Law but through faith in Christ Jesus, even we have believed in Christ Jesus, that we may be justified by faith in Christ, and not by the works of the Law; since by the works of the Law shall no flesh be justified" (Gal 2:16).

This matter is so serious for Paul that he vigorously denounces legalism — whether through ceremonial fastidiousness or legalistic accomplishment: "I do not nullify the grace of God; for if righteousness comes through the Law, then Christ died needlessly" (Gal 2:21).

The negative impression regarding the Law in Galatians has no bearing on the continuing validity of God's Law as a moral guide in the new covenant era. It simply counters the Judaizers' use of the Law as an instrument of salvation.

John 1:17

Another passage sometimes employed by those who dismiss God's Law is John 1:17. Early in John's Gospel he writes:

> For the Law was given through Moses; grace and truth were realized
> through Jesus Christ.

Some believe this pits the Law against grace and truth. And since we are
in the new covenant and under God's grace, the Law no longer prevails.
This is a Class 4 passage: it is simply misunderstood.

We should note that even on the very surface this statement does not
in any way render the Law null and void. Nothing disparaging is said of
the Law. What is disparaging about the Law being "given through Moses"? After all, is not Moses the Lord's special "servant" (Exo 14:31; Deut
34:5; Josh 1:1–2; Neh 1:7; Psa 105:26; Mal 4:4; etc.[3]) whom God praises
as such (Num 12:7–8)? Does not Ezra deem him "the man of God" (Ezra
3:2)? Does not God himself speak highly of Moses as an example of
righteousness when he declares: "even though Moses and Samuel were
to stand before Me, My heart would not be with this people" (Jer 15:1)?

Jesus even declares Moses' writings as more powerful than the mir-
acle of resurrection (Luke 16:29–31). He also uses Moses as a prophetic
witness to his own ministry (Luke 24:27; cp. Luke 16:23; John 5:46).

If we carefully consider John 1:17 we will note that John does not set
the Law [*nomos*] over against "grace and truth" [*hē charis kai he alētheia*],
as if they were opposites or contradictory. If he did, this would imply the
God's revelation in the Law is both non-gracious and false. Contrary to
such a prospect we have seen that the Law is given in the context of
God's gracious dealings with Israel (Exo 20:2). Interestingly, in the Septu-
agint (the Greek version of the Old Testament) Moses asks God: "How
will it be truly [*alēthios*] known that I have found grace [*charin*] with you?"
(Exo 33:16). Grace and truth surround Moses himself.

Furthermore, contrary to such a tendency, the Psalmist declares:
"Your law is truth" (Psa 119:142) and "all Your commandments are truth"
(Psa 119:151). In the New Testament Paul himself teaches that the Law "is
the embodiment of knowledge and truth" (Rom 2:20). Thus, neither the
Old Testament nor the New Testament deem the Law as without grace
and truth.

---

[3] Joshua indicates Moses' high esteem as the servant of God. He records
God's calling Moses "My servant" (Josh 1:2, 7, 13, 15). When Joshua refers to
Moses he honorifically titles him as "God's servant," "the servant of God," or "the
servant of the Lord" (Josh 1:1; 8:31, 33; 9:24; 11:12, 15; 12:6; 13:8; 14:7; 22:2,
4–5).

So then, what is going on in John 1:17? We should note that rather than contrasting the nouns (*nomos* v. *charis* and *alētheia*), John actually contrasts the verbs. We know this not only from the particular verbs employed but by their placement in the sentence. John states that the Law was *given* [*edothē*] through Moses (i.e., it is not his own); grace and truth are actually *realized* [*egeneto*] in Christ (i.e., it is his own). Structurally the two parts of this verse present the verbs in the last position, thereby emphasizing them. We may literally translate the text: "The law through Moses was given; the grace and truth through Jesus Christ became." As great as Moses is, he is nevertheless simply the deliverer of the Law, not its source. Christ, however, is himself the very embodiment of God's grace and truth. This is John's point.

New Testament scholars deem John's Gospel as one of the most Judaic writings of the New Testament. In this highly Judaic Gospel the Apostle sets Jesus over against all the institutions of Israel.[4] Most technical commentaries will note how John's Gospel:

> is enriched by an extraordinarily frequent and subtle number of *allusions* to the Old Testament. One of the features of these allusions is the manner in which Jesus is assumed to *replace* Old Testament figures and institutions. He is the new temple, the one of whom Moses wrote, the true bread from heaven, the true Son, the genuine vine, the tabernacle, the serpent in the wilderness, the passover. Rarely articulated, there is nevertheless an underlying *hermeneutic* at work, a way of reading the Old Testament that goes back to Jesus himself.[5]

As we may now understand, in John 1:17 the Apostle is stating that Christ's role in redemptive history excels that of Moses who is merely a message deliverer. "Grace and truth" are actually "realized through Jesus Christ." This is because Christ directly manifests God as his "exact representation" (Heb 1:3) for "He is the image of the invisible God" (Col 1:16). This is the very point with which John opens: "In the beginning was the Word, and the Word was with God, and the Word was God" (John 1:1). Thus, "grace and truth" are expressly associated with the Incarnate Lord:

---

[4] The Epistle the Hebrews is designed to make the same point, though in a more obvious way.

[5] D. A. Carson, *The Gospel according to John* (Grand Rapids: Eerdmans, 1991), 98. Cf. R. Alan Culpepper in Bieringer, R. D. Pollefeyt, and F. Vandecasteele -Vanneuville, *Anti-Judaism and the Fourth Gospel* (Louisville: Westminster John Knox, 2001), 88–93.

"And the Word became flesh, and dwelt among us, and we beheld His glory, glory as of the only begotten from the Father, full of grace and truth" (John 1:14).

So then, nothing in John 1:17 diminishes the Law as our abiding ethical standard. This verse is wholly misunderstood and misused when employed against the continuing relevance of God's Law.

The ceremonial law

The ceremonial law is often brought forward to undermine a proper exposition of Matthew 5:17–19, as given in chapter 3 above. Opponents will argue that my exposition of Matthew 5 requires the continuing validity of even the ceremonial and ritual features of the Law. After all, I have pointed out that Jesus declared: "For truly I say to you, until heaven and earth pass away, not the smallest letter or stroke shall pass away from the Law, until all is accomplished" (Matt 5:18). This appears to require that we must continue the animal sacrifices, ritual circumcision, ceremonial cleansings, and so forth.

On the surface this seems to be a potent response. But looks are deceiving: this argument is not a rebuttal of my exposition of Matthew 5. Used in this fallacious way it would be a rebuttal of *Christ himself*. After all, Christ is the one who proclaims "until heaven and earth pass away, not the smallest letter or stroke shall pass away from the Law" (Matt 5:18).

So, how *do* we understand the cessation of the ceremonial features of the Law *while* maintaining that continuing validity of even the smallest elements in the Law?

In answering this, we must recognize first that God's Law reflects two sorts of truth: moral and restorative. That is, the Law reflects God's holy justice as well as his gracious salvation. Thus, it embodies righteous directives and promises gracious redemption. The moral features of the Law reflect the one reality and the ceremonial features reflect the other. But how does this help us understand Christ's strong statement in Matthew 5:18?

Here we must recognize that *by design* the ceremonial law is never intended to be an end in itself. It is always prophetically and typologically forward-looking, anticipating the coming of the Redeemer and the finalization of salvation through his work. The ceremonial law foreshadowed the eternal truths of Christ's work. God intended it to be superseded:

Now if perfection was through the Levitical priesthood (for on the basis of it the people received the Law), what further need was there for another priest to arise according to the order of Melchizedek, and not be designated according to the order of Aaron? For when the priesthood is changed, of necessity there takes place a change of law also. (Heb 7: 11–12)

Secondly, as the ceremonial laws expects, Christ's coming confirms their essential meaning and eternally validates their redemptive truth. Christ is the reality of which they are but the shadow. Thus, for us to keep the ceremonial laws today in the same way ancient Israel kept them in the old covenant would actually breach them. To continue engaging in the ceremonies would effectively deny that they point ahead to their fulfillment, which necessitates their expiration.

Thirdly, rather than simply being rejected, however, the ceremonies were observed for us by Christ and their prophetic realities were lived out in him. The Lord Jesus did not destroy or remove their meaning, he lived them out for us thereby making their *way* of being kept irrelevant. *He* is our sacrifice (1 Cor 5:7; cp. John 1:29; 1 Pet 1:19). We do not keep the ceremonial and prophetic features of the Law today because Christ has lived them out for us — according to their very design.

Sometimes we may find it difficult to determine what laws are ceremonial and what ones are not. But this does not destroy the principle of the continuing relevance of God's Law. After all, in various places in Scripture we will find some things difficult to comprehend — as do Peter (2 Pet 3:16) and John (Rev 17:6b–7). But this difficulty should not cause us to discount those verses. Rather, it should spur us to deeper study to gain fuller understanding of God's word.

Conclusion

In this book I am arguing for the continuing validity of God's Law in the new covenant era even into our own modern times. I have presented evidence from the Old Testament and the New Testament, from Christ himself and from his apostles. A strong biblical case supports the relevance of God's Law.

As in virtually every biblical doctrine, difficult verses exist and must be explained, even on such fundamental doctrines as the Trinity and the deity of Christ. Our view of the integrity of Scripture forces us to reflect on the apparently discordant verses. In this chapter I focused on several biblical arguments urged against continuing God's Law. In each case we saw that the evidence brought against the Law may be answered, so that our positive evidence for it remains.

Chapter 6

THE WORLD-SCOPE OF GOD'S LAW

In this chapter I will consider the question of the wider obligation to God's Law. I will focus on its application beyond the Church and in the world at large. To engage this issue we must consider the question regarding:

God's Law and Israel

An objection we frequently hear brought against God's Law is that it was expressly designed for use only by old covenant Israel and even intended to be applied only in its ancient setting. Were this true, its relevance would be limited to the special redemptive nation of Israel in pre-Christian times and for no other nation in any other time. Dispensationalists are especially prone to use this argument quite vigorously: "The stipulations of Sinai were not for the nations in general but to a people under grace.... Since nations around Israel were not called to adopt the Mosaic Covenant, it seems evident that the pagan nations would not be judged by the law of Moses."[1]

But though this might be expected of dispensationalism with its severe compartmentalization of history, some reformed theologians even take a dispensational approach to the matter, as well. Such a compartmentalist argument is clearly visible in the following reformed statement:

> Israel as a nation was chosen by God "out of all the peoples on the face of the earth to be his people, his treasured possession" (Dt 7:6). No other nation of the ancient or modern world is like Israel in its place in redemptive history. . . . Before we can apply a case law from the Old Testament today, therefore, we must consider not only cultural adaptations but also discontinuities that result because of the difference in redemptive status between Israel and any modern society.[2]

How shall we respond to such approaches?

---

[1] H. Wayne House and Thomas D. Ice, *Dominion Theology: Blessing or Curse?* (Portland, Ore.: Multnomah, 1988),128, 129.

[2] Will S. Barker and W. Robert Godfrey, *Theonomy: An Informed Critique* (Grand Rapids: Zondervan, 1990) 47, 48.

Mosaic Law and the Nations

The basic argument

I will briefly cite a few counter-responses to this objection. These should quickly expose the flaw in this approach to the biblical evidence.

1. The objection confuses moral commandments and covenantal form. We must understand that moral commands are distinguishable from the covenantal system in which they are found. For example, in both the new covenant and the old covenant, we find commands obligating us to love father and mother (Deut 5:16 and Eph 6:2), even though the old covenant rationale is that "your days may be prolonged in the land which the Lord you God gives you." Indeed, both covenants — though structurally different and covenantally distinct — forbid murder (Exo 20:13; Rom 1:29), fornication (Exo 20:14; Rom 13:9), theft (Exo 20:15; 1 Cor 6:9–10), and so forth. This does not mean that by affirming the continuity of moral commands from the old covenant into the new we identify the two covenants as if no differences whatsoever distinguish them.

The old covenant structure and ceremonial obligations, which included the sacrificial system and various ritual and typological features, is established only with Israel. Yet it was established on a moral substructure rooted in the unchanging righteousness of God which promoted perpetually obligatory commandments of God. Ethical requirements may be distinguished from the historical and redemptive trappings in which they are found. Moral commandments are justice-defining and are distinguishable from ceremonial laws that are redemption-expounding. As evidence for this we may note the Old Testament itself.

In Hosea 6:6 God contrasts moral and ceremonial obligations: "For I delight in loyalty rather than sacrifice, / And in the knowledge of God rather than burnt offerings." We witness the same in 1 Samuel 15:22: "Has the Lord as much delight in burnt offerings and sacrifices / As in obeying the voice of the Lord? / Behold, to obey is better than sacrifice, / And to heed than the fat of rams." King David affirms this in Psalm 51:14–17:

> Deliver me from bloodguiltiness, O God, the God of my salvation; / Then my tongue will joyfully sing of Your righteousness. / O Lord, open my lips, / That my mouth may declare Your praise. / For You do not delight in sacrifice, otherwise I would give it; / You are not pleased with burnt offering. / The sacrifices of God are a broken spirit; / A broken and a contrite heart, O God, You will not despise.

We can find many Old Testament samples of God elevating moral and spiritual obligations over ceremonial fidelity (e.g., Psa 40:6; Prov 21:3; Isa 1:10–17; Mic 6:7–8). But we never discover the opposite in either testament. God never tolerates murder while encouraging ceremonial fidelity.

2. God's Law is in fact designed to be a model for the nations. As Israel finally prepares to enter the Promised Land to undertake her own place among the nations of the world, Moses speaks to her about God's Law:

> See, I have taught you statutes and judgments just as the Lord my God commanded me, that you should do thus in the land where you are entering to possess it. So keep and do them, *for that is your wisdom and your understanding in the sight of the peoples who will hear all these statutes and say, "Surely this great nation is a wise and understanding people."* For what great nation is there that has a god so near to it as is the Lord our God whenever we call on Him? Or what great nation is there that has statutes and judgments as righteous as this whole law which I am setting before you today? (Deut 4:5–8)

God graciously gives his Law to Israel as a corporate, national body so that she might soon be established as a political state on the world stage. In fact, many elements in his Law apply *only* to the political-judicial sphere, such as laws establishing capital punishment (Exo 21:12), pecuniary fines (Exo 21:19, 36), property rights (Exo 22:8), and so forth. The many statutes included in the Law are to govern the people corporately as they inhabit the Land to formally establish a state: "And now, O Israel, listen to the statutes and the judgments which I am teaching you to perform, in order that you may live and go in and take possession of the land which the Lord, the God of your fathers, is giving you" (Deut 4:1).

In that God is establishing Israel as a nation and equipping her with his Law, this is for her corporate good as a nation in the historical long-run:

> So you shall keep His statutes and His commandments which I am giving you today, that it may go well with you and with your children after you, and that you may live long on the land which the Lord your God is giving you for all time. (Deut 4:40)

> Be careful to listen to all these words which I command you, in order that it may be well with you and your sons after you forever, for you will be doing what is good and right in the sight of the Lord your God. (Deut 12:28)

This is repeated over and over in Deuteronomy (cf. Deut 4:1; 5:16, 29, 33; 6:3, 18; 8:1; 16:20; 22:7; 30:16, 19).

But if Israel despises God's Law, this will result in her political collapse and social ruin under God's wrath and curse:

> But it shall come about, if you will not obey the Lord your God, to observe to do all His commandments and His statutes with which I charge you today, that all these curses shall come upon you and overtake you. . . . The Lord will bring a nation against you from afar, from the end of the earth, as the eagle swoops down, a nation whose language you shall not understand, a nation of fierce countenance who shall have no respect for the old, nor show favor to the young. . . . And it shall come about that as the Lord delighted over you to prosper you, and multiply you, so the Lord will delight over you to make you perish and destroy you; and you shall be torn from the land where you are entering to possess it. Moreover, the Lord will scatter you among all peoples, from one end of the earth to the other end of the earth; and there you shall serve other gods, wood and stone, which you or your fathers have not known. And among those nations you shall find no rest, and there shall be no resting place for the sole of your foot; but there the Lord will give you a trembling heart, failing of eyes, and despair of soul. (Deut 28:15, 49–50, 63–65)

The Law is designed to bring blessings upon Israel and to prevent her ruin as a nation. This also is repeated frequently in the Old Testament: Leviticus 26:14–43; Joshua 23:15; Daniel 9:11.

Though many reasons obligate Israel to keep God's Law, the Deuteronomy 4 passage cited above focuses on her duty to be a model for the nations. When she enters into Canaan she will establish herself as a nation by God's grace (Exo 20:1–2; cp. Deut 5:6). God expects her to live according to his judicial standards so that she might be an example to the pagan nations. After all, God calls her corporately to be a "kingdom of priests" to the world: "Now then, if you will indeed obey My voice and keep My covenant, then you shall be My own possession among all the peoples, for all the earth is Mine; and you shall be to Me a kingdom of priests and a holy nation" (Exo 19:5–6). When the nations see her as "wise and understanding" they will recognize her "statutes and judgments as righteous" (Deut 4:6, 8) and be moved to emulate her law system for their own good.

This modeling is for the good of the pagan nations, for God is "a great King over all the earth" (Psa 47:2, 7) and "chastens the nations" (Psa 94:10). The whole earth is to rejoice that "the Lord reigns" because "righteousness and justice are the foundation of His throne" (Psa 97:1–2). His law presents his "justice for a light of the peoples" (Isa 51:4). Therefore,

God's statutes must be taught to earth's kings (Psa 119:46; cp. Psa 2: 10–12; Isa 2:2–3; Mic 4:2) for God judges the wicked of the earth "who wander from Your statutes" (Psa 119:118). The wicked pollute the earth when they break God's Law: "The earth is also polluted by its inhabitants, for they transgressed laws, violated statutes, broke the everlasting covenant" (Isa 24:5).

Since Israel's law is *God's* Law for her as a society and a nation, should we not assume that he has ordained it as a righteous standard (Psa 19:9)? And if the judicial and political elements in God's Law were righteous then, why are they not righteous now? Is not God's righteousness unchanging, enduring forever (Psa 111:3; 112:9; 119:142, 144, 160; Isa 51: 8)?

3. The nations around Israel are often judged for breaching God's moral standards, but never for breaching the Mosaic covenantal form. We see this in God's warning to Israel as she prepares to enter the Land to be established as a nation:

> Do not defile yourselves by any of these things; for by all these the nations which I am casting out before you have become defiled. For the land has become defiled, therefore I have visited its punishment upon it, so the land has spewed out its inhabitants. But as for you, you are to keep My statutes and My judgments, and shall not do any of these abominations, neither the native, nor the alien who sojourns among you (for the men of the land who have been before you have done all these abominations, and the land has become defiled). (Lev 18:24–27)

The things he is speaking about here include such immoral conduct as incest (Deut 18:6–17), polygamy (18:18[3]), adultery (18:20), idolatry (18:21), homosexuality (18:22), and bestiality (18:23).

In other places we see God's applying judgments against nations for breaching his moral, not his ceremonial legislation. In Amos 1:6 Gaza was judged for kidnaping (Exo 21:16; Deut 24:7). In Habakkuk 2:6 Babylon was judged for financial plunder (Exo 22:25–27; Deut 24:6, 10–13). But nowhere do we see a nation judged for ceremonial failures.

---

[3] Israel repeatedly breached the law against polygamy. But here God prohibits taking a woman in addition to another woman (the word "sister" simply means another woman). From the beginning God intended monogamy (Gen 2:24). Because of Israel's prior practice of polygamy, though, God imposes legislation on the fair treatment of secondary wives (Deut 21:15–17) rather than requiring the marriage already effected be disrupted and one of the wives be cast out.

Because God is unchanging and his righteousness is everlasting we
see this same corporate judgment operating earlier in Abraham's day —
even before the Law is written down on tables of stone. There we see
God's judgment of Sodom and Gomorrah due to their being overrun with
rampant homosexual conduct (Deut 19:4–8; cp. Jude 1:7) which is con-
demned in God's Law (Lev 18:22; 20:13; Deut 23:17; 1 Kgs 22:46). Sodom
and Gomorrah are committed to "lawless deeds" (2 Pet 2:8) so that their
judgment becomes a paradigmatic warning of God's wrath upon lawless
peoples.[4] The angels who visit Abraham warn him: "we are about to
destroy this place, because their outcry has become so great before the
Lord that the Lord has sent us to destroy it" (Gen 19:13, 24). The angels
do not condemn Sodom and Gomorrah for not practicing circumcision or
offering sacrifices.

4. *Church and State are separate in the Old Testament era.* Despite the
close working relationship between Church and State in the Old Testament (after all, they were both subject to God), they are nevertheless
distinct entities. God firmly and clearly distinguishes between Israel's civil
ruler and her priestly head. He appoints Moses over civil matters and
Aaron over priestly matters (Exo 16:33–34; 29:1ff). Thus, at the very foundation of Israel's national existence God carefully separates the priestly
and the civil functions in Israel's formative leaders.

Later in Israel's experience we see the continuation of this practice
of separating the offices of priest and king. In a society where Church and
State are united we might expect that the civil and the priestly offices
would be merged into one individual. But in Israel they are not. For
example, in 2 Chronicles 19:11 we read:

> And behold, Amariah the chief priest will be over you in all that pertains
> to the Lord; and Zebadiah the son of Ishmael, the ruler of the house of
> Judah, in all that pertains to the king. Also the Levites shall be officers
> before you. Act resolutely, and the Lord be with the upright.

Indeed, we discover God judging Israel's kings who breach this separation of powers. In 1 Samuel 13:8–14 Samuel rebukes Saul for presenting a priestly offering instead of waiting for Samuel to do so. Samuel
declares that because of his action Saul's "kingdom shall not endure" for
God would seek "a man after his own heart" to appoint "as ruler over His

---

[4] See: Deut 29:23, 32; 32:32; Isa 1:9–10; 3:9; 13:19; Jer 23:14; 49:18; 50:40;
Lam 4:6; Eze 16:46–49, 53, 55; Amos 4:11; Zeph 2:9; Matt 10:15; 11:23–24; Luke
10:12; 17:29; Rom 9:29; 2 Pet 2:6–8; Jude 7; Rev 11:8.

people, because you have not kept what the Lord commanded you" (1 Sam 13:14).

In 2 Chronicles we see King Uzziah judged because "his heart was so proud that he acted corruptly, and he was unfaithful to the Lord his God, for he entered the temple of the Lord to burn incense on the altar of incense" (2 Chron 26:16). The priests oppose him warning "it is not for you, Uzziah, to burn incense to the Lord, but for the priests, the sons of Aaron who are consecrated to burn incense. Get out of the sanctuary, for you have been unfaithful, and will have no honor from the Lord God" (2 Chron 26:18). When he takes up the burning of incense God strikes him with leprosy (2 Chron 26:19–21).

As another marker of the distinction between Church and State, Scripture records Israel's building a house for the king, i.e., a palace (1 Kgs 6:1—7:12) that was separate from the house for God, i.e, the temple (1 Kgs 7:13–51).

5. People from all nations are under obligation to God's Law today. As demonstrated in earlier chapters, God's Law is a standard for the nations at all times and in all places. I have established much positive evidence from both testaments to this end. But in this chapter I need to rehearse a little of this to fill out the argument now before us.

Paul's writings are very clear in this regard: "although they know the ordinance of God, that those who practice such things are worthy of death, they not only do the same, but also give hearty approval to those who practice them" (Rom 1:32). Here the internal God-created witness (Rom 1:18–19) recognizes that "the ordinance of God" deems some crimes as "worthy of death." A few verses later he writes:

> For all who have sinned without the Law will also perish without the Law; and all who have sinned under the Law will be judged by the Law; for not the hearers of the Law are just before God, but the doers of the Law will be justified. For when Gentiles who do not have the Law do instinctively the things of the Law, these, not having the Law, are a law to themselves, in that they show the work of the Law written in their hearts, their conscience bearing witness, and their thoughts alternately accusing or else defending them. (Rom 2:12–15)

We find a very clear statement by Paul in Romans 3:19: "Now we know that whatever the Law says, it speaks to those who are under the Law, that every mouth may be closed, and all the world may become accountable to God (cf. Rom 12:19–13:10). He states later in his ministry that God's Law comports with the gospel message and remains obligatory as "sound doctrine":

But we know that the Law is good, if one uses it lawfully, realizing the fact that law is not made for a righteous man, but for those who are lawless and rebellious, for the ungodly and sinners, for the unholy and profane, for those who kill their fathers or mothers, for murderers and immoral men and homosexuals and kidnappers and liars and perjurers, and whatever else is contrary to sound teaching, according to the glorious gospel of the blessed God, with which I have been entrusted. (1 Tim 1:8–11)

We should expect this in light of the Messiah's coming in the first century, for he is to teach the nations God's Law:

Now it will come about that / In the last days, / The mountain of the house of the Lord / Will be established as the chief of the mountains, / And will be raised above the hills; / And all the nations will stream to it. / And many peoples will come and say, "Come, let us go up to the mountain of the Lord, / To the house of the God of Jacob; / That He may teach us concerning His ways, / And that we may walk in His paths." / For the law will go forth from Zion, / And the word of the Lord from Jerusalem. (Isa 2:2–3; cp. Mic 4:1–3)

Consequently, Paul considers God's Law in our era to be "just" (Rom 7:12) and "good" (Rom 7:12; 1 Tim 1:8). The New Testament views it as the "unalterable" standard for providing "just recompense" for "every transgression and disobedience" (Heb 2:2).

A Potential Problem

Oftentimes Christians object to the modern application of God's Law because they believe it would impose capital punishment for apostasy. Deuteronomy 13 and 17 would seem to require capital punishment for Jehovah's Witnesses, Mormons, and other cult members. For instance, Deuteronomy 13:10 applies to false prophets: "You shall stone him to death because he has sought to seduce you from the Lord your God who brought you out from the land of Egypt, out of the house of slavery" (Deut 13:10).

How does the modern advocate of God's Law understand these capital sanctions as recorded in Deuteronomy 13:1–18 and 17:2–7? This an important question. I will set forth some critical observations regarding the application of these laws when properly interpreted.

First, it should be noted at the outset that the framing of the law in Deuteronomy 13 has in view *solicitation and seduction to idolatry* (Deut 13:2, 6, 13). It does not have in mind doctrinal error, personal unbelief, or even personal rejection of faith in Jehovah God. Those who mistakenly assume that this law would inevitably draw the State's sword into church discipline for unbelief are mistaken. In point of fact, unbelief in Israel is *not* punishable by death. For one to refuse to be circumcised (an expression of unbelief, cf. Lev 26:41; Deut 30:6; Jer 9:25–26; Eze 44:7) means that he was "cut off" from the religious community (Gen 17:14). Therefore, he is excluded from the worship gatherings in Israel (Exo 12:48; Eze 44:7, 9); he is not capitally punished.

Second, Deuteronomy 13 actually is framing a law against *treason*. This is evident on the basis of the following three-staged consideration: (1) By the very nature of the case, the *god* of a society is that society's source of law.[5] It has been thus in the fallen world since the temptation of Adam and Eve to be as "God" by "knowing" (determining, legislating) good and evil (Gen. 3:5). Hence, the pagan tendency for political rulers to be deified, as illustrated in the Babylonian king (Isa 14:4, 13–14) and the Roman emperor (Matt 22:15–22; 2 Thess 2:4; Rev 13:4ff). Hegel clothed this pagan conception in modern dress: "The State is the Divine Idea as it exists on Earth."[6] To seek another god, therefore, is to turn from the Law of the present God, Jehovah, which Law is the constitutional basis of the nation of Israel.

(2) The context preceding Deuteronomy 13 speaks of the gods of the nations around Israel. It speaks of *nations serving their gods*: "When the Lord your God cuts off before you the nations which you are going in to dispossess, and you dispossess them and dwell in their land, beware that you are not ensnared to follow them, after they are destroyed before you, and that you do not inquire after their gods, saying, 'How do these nations serve their gods, *that I also may do likewise?*'" (Deut 12:29–30). This leads me to note that:

(3) The Deuteronomic law is developed in such a way as to indicate the *ultimate outcome* of such apostasy. It is wholesale, treasonous rebellion against the lawful authority and integrity of the nation: "If you hear in one of your cities, which the Lord your God is giving you to live in, anyone saying that some worthless men have gone out from among you and have seduced the inhabitants of their city, saying, 'Let us go and serve other gods' (whom you have not known). . ." (Deut 13:12–13). As

---

[5] See R. J. Rushdoony, *The One and the Many: Studies in the Philosophy of Order and Ultimacy* (Fairfax, Vir.: Thoburn, 1971).

[6] Georg Wilhelm Friedrich Hegel, *Philosophy of History*, trans. by J. Sibree (New York: Collier, 1901), 87.

commentator Craigie puts it: "In its implications, the crime would be equivalent to treason or espionage in time of war."[7] Thus, in an important respect such a law is a right to "self-defense" for the nation, as is the right to wage defensive warfare.

Third, any perception of idolatry as a quietistic unbelief is wholly mistaken. The very nature of idolatry involves the ancient worshiper in a number of capital crimes. *Thus, the punishment for idolatry is a punishment for those particular crimes.* As Mayes notes, Deuteronomy 12:29–32 is the "general introduction" to chapter 13.[8] This "general introduction" clearly speaks of certain "abominable acts" of idol worshipers:

> When the Lord your God cuts off before you the nations which you are going in to dispossess, and you dispossess them and dwell in their land, beware that you are not ensnared to follow them, after they are destroyed before you, and that you do not inquire after their gods, saying, "How do these nations serve their gods, that I also may do likewise?" You shall not behave thus toward the Lord your God, for every abominable act which the Lord hates they have done for their gods; for they even burn their sons and daughters in the fire to their gods. (Deut 12:29–31)

Idolatry involves wide-scale criminal conduct and is a dangerous cancer.[9] The Canaanites are not thrust out of the land for unbelief, but for wholesale moral and criminal perversion.[10] That idolatry is a real danger is evident in the days of Israel's apostasy, when abominable acts are committed (2 Kgs 16:3; 21:6; 23:10; Jer 7:31–32; 19:4–6). All nations serve idols in those days (2 Kgs 17:29). Israel falls right in with them — *and* with their grossly immoral crimes (2 Kgs 17:7ff, 17–19). This corrupts and subverts the moral fiber of their culture by encouraging child sacrifice, bestiality, homosexual conduct, cult prostitution, and the like.

Thus, as we have seen, the apostasy laws in God's Law do not punish mere unbelief or misguided worship. Those laws were designed to protect *the legal integrity of the nation* (criminalizing such actions as treason, conspiracy, seditious revolt, and espionage) and to bring *judgment against*

---

[7] Peter C. Craigie, *The Book of Deuteronomy* (Grand Rapids: Eerdmans, 1976), 222.

[8] A. D. H. Mayes, *Deuteronomy* (Grand Rapids: Eerdmans, 1979), 230.

[9] See Lev 18:21–30; Rom 1:21–32. 1 Cor 10:20 shows the connection with Satan worship.

[10] See: Lev 18:3, 24ff; 20:23; Deut 9:5; 18:9–12.

wicked idolatry (criminalizing such actions as cultural subversion and public mayhem).[11]

Conclusion

Though God expressly reveals his Law to Israel, he does so in order that Israel would be an example to the nations. Many Scripture passages show that the Law of God applies beyond the borders of Israel, even extending beyond her ancient times and into the future. In fact, were we to remove the Law because it is given to an ancient culture, then we should remove Christianity's New Testament moral directives because they were given in an only slightly less ancient setting some 2000 years ago.

Paul is clear in this regard: "Now we know that whatever the Law says, it speaks to those who are under the Law, that every mouth may be closed, and all the world may become accountable to God" (Rom 3:19). Those "under the Law" include "every mouth" and "all the world."

---

[11] The false prophet in Deuteronomy 13:5 is not just a foolish mouther of error, but is a focus point for agitating the masses to rebellion. The prophets of Israel "demanded that same obedience to their words as was due to the Law of God." E. J. Young, *Introduction to the Old Testament* (Grand Rapids: Eerdmans, 1964), p. 34. The false prophets would tend to mirror the cultural function of the true prophets, and were, thus, dangerous as conspirators.

Chapter 7

PRACTICAL BENEFITS OF GOD'S LAW

In that the Law is in fact *God's* Law, it is practical. Paul's global statement regarding Scripture applies to the Law which is included in Scripture: "All Scripture [including the Law] is profitable" (2 Tim 3:16a). In this chapter I will highlight a few random samples of the Law's practicality. In that most Christians today decry the Law as not only outmoded but downright burdensome, these benefits should encourage us to see that the opposite is true. As Christians we should affirm the Apostle John's statement: "For this is the love of God, that we keep His commandments; and His commandments *are not burdensome*" (1 John 5:3).

When men strive to keep God's Law hoping to meritoriously earn salvation, then it does become a burden. In Acts 15:1 some converted Pharisees are teaching that "unless you are circumcised according to the custom of Moses, you cannot be saved" (Acts 15:1). Peter rejects this approach, noting: "Now therefore why do you put God to the test by placing upon the neck of the disciples a yoke which neither our fathers nor we have been able to bear?" (Acts 15:10).

But when the Law is used as God intended, then it is a blessing. In the longest Psalm in Scripture, the psalmist declares his love for the Law: "O how I love Your law! / It is my meditation all the day" (Psa 119:97; cp. 113), noting that "those who love Your law have great peace" (Psa 119: 165).

Scriptural Benefits

One of the most immediate benefits of affirming God's Law is that we are left with an intact word of God. The Christian should not enter into Scripture with the presupposition that certain parts must be cast aside unless repeated in the New Testament. Rather, our approach should be one which allows only a word from God in Scripture itself to set aside any portion of Scripture. For instance, the Book of Hebrews clearly sets aside the sacrificial system (as having accomplished its purpose in pointing to Christ as the Redeemer):

> The Holy Spirit is signifying this, that the way into the holy place has not yet been disclosed, while the outer tabernacle is still standing, which is a symbol for the present time. Accordingly both gifts and sacrifices are

offered which cannot make the worshiper perfect in conscience, since they relate only to food and drink and various washings, regulations for the body imposed until a time of reformation. But when Christ appeared as a high priest of the good things to come, He entered through the greater and more perfect tabernacle, not made with hands, that is to say, not of this creation; and not through the blood of goats and calves, but through His own blood, He entered the holy place once for all, having obtained eternal redemption. (Heb 9:8–12)

For the adherent to God's Law, the Bible is left intact as a unified word from God that is relevant for all times. Not only so but this approach to the Law affirms Scripture's non-contradictory nature. The positive affirmations of God's Law by Jesus and Paul, for instance, do not contradict the Christian theological system by both endorsing and dismissing God's Law: "Do not think that I came to abolish the Law or the Prophets; I did not come to abolish, but to fulfill" (Matt 5:17). "Do we then nullify the Law through faith? May it never be! On the contrary, we establish the Law" (Rom 3:31).

As we engage the practical benefits of the Law further, we must understand that much of God's revelation of his Law comes by way of "case-law." Case-laws provide particular, concrete illustrations of the application of God's moral standards. These are specific applications relevant to concrete historical circumstances which serve to demonstrate how the Law should be applied in other similar contexts. These case-laws are not limited to the express situations presented.

Personal Benefits

God's Law promises practical benefits for the individual living according to its directives. We may see this in just a few random samples.

1. God's Law outlines specific moral behavior. Thus, it eliminates guesswork from moral conduct. "Thy word is a lamp to my feet, / And a light to my path" (Psa 119:105). The Christian should not be one who gropes in darkness, but one who walks in the light (1 John 1:7). Thus, God's Law keeps us from stumbling morally by informing us of God's will for "How blessed are those whose way is blameless, / Who walk in the law of the Lord" (Psa 119:1). We read of the righteous man: "How blessed is the man who does not walk in the counsel of the wicked, / Nor stand in the path of sinners, / Nor sit in the seat of scoffers! / But his delight is in the law of the Lord, / And in His law he meditates day and night" (Psa1:1–2).

The father in the home should live by and promote God's Law in his daily life and for the good of his family:

And you shall love the Lord your God with all your heart and with all your soul and with all your might. And these words, which I am commanding you today, shall be on your heart; and you shall teach them diligently to your sons and shall talk of them when you sit in your house and when you walk by the way and when you lie down and when you rise up. And you shall bind them as a sign on your hand and they shall be as frontals on your forehead. And you shall write them on the doorposts of your house and on your gates. (Deut 6:5–9)

2. God's Law obligates us to love our neighbor. This use of the Law encourages pleasant, harmonious inter-personal relations: "You shall love your neighbor as yourself" (Lev 19:18b). In fact, this law serves as one of the leading summary principles of God's Law. Jesus teaches us: "'You shall love the Lord your God with all your heart, and with all your soul, and with all your mind.' This is the great and foremost commandment. The second is like it, 'You shall love your neighbor as yourself.' On these two commandments depend the whole Law and the Prophets" (Matt 22:37–40). The New Testament frequently repeats this law (Matt 19:19; Mark 12:31; Luke 10:27; Rom 13:9; Gal 5:14), even calling it "the royal law" (Jms 2:8).

3. God's Law requires us to treat our enemies respectfully. In Exodus 23:4–5 we read: "If you meet your enemy's ox or his donkey wandering away, you shall surely return it to him. If you see the donkey of one who hates you lying helpless under its load, you shall refrain from leaving it to him, you shall surely release it with him." Leviticus 19:18 commands: "You shall not take vengeance, nor bear any grudge against the sons of your people, but you shall love your neighbor as yourself; I am the Lord."

The wisdom literature applying this law frequently expands upon it. Proverbs commands: "Do not rejoice when your enemy falls, / And do not let your heart be glad when he stumbles; / Lest the Lord see it and be displeased, / And He turn away His anger from him" (Prov 24:17–18). The Book of Job asks: "Have I rejoiced at the extinction of my enemy, / Or exulted when evil befell him? (Job 31:29). When men hold God's Law in high regard it reduces personal vengeance and enhances social stability.

4. God's Law expects us to insure the safety of others. It speaks particularly of guests on our property. Deuteronomy 22:8 commands: "When you build a new house, then you shall make a parapet for your roof, that you may not bring bloodguilt on your house if anyone falls from it." In fact, this is not only a moral obligation but a civil one as we see in a parallel case law: "If a man opens a pit, or digs a pit and does not cover it over, and an ox or a donkey falls into it, the owner of the pit shall make restitution; he shall give money to its owner, and the dead animal shall become his" (Exo 21:33–34).

5. God's Law expects us to pay for harm we cause. It does so by obligating us to fully compensate those whom we harm. Exodus 21:18–19 warns: "If men contend with each other, and one strikes the other with a stone or with his fist, and he does not die but is confined to his bed, if he rises again and walks about outside with his staff, then he who struck him shall be acquitted. He shall only pay for the loss of his time, and shall provide for him to be thoroughly healed."

6. God's Law forbids interest-bearing loans to the needy. We read in Exodus 22:25–27: "If you lend money to any of My people who are poor among you, you shall not be like a moneylender to him; you shall not charge him interest. If you ever take your neighbor's garment as a pledge, you shall return it to him before the sun goes down. For that is his only covering, it is his garment for his skin. What will he sleep in? And it will be that when he cries to Me, I will hear, for I am gracious." This case law protects the needy from unscrupulous oppression.

I could present many other case law samples, but these should suffice as illustrations of the practical beauty and applicability of God's Law. In the conclusion of this chapter I will suggest some larger books that will provide great detail along these lines.

Public Benefits

The Law of God is not simply a system of personal morality, but also reveals to us a corporate morality covering the social, political, and judicial spheres as well.

General benefits

1. God's Law provides an unchanging foundation for society. In the self-consciously Christian approach to social ethics, an unchanging Law becomes the basis of social order, rather than the changing whims of legislators, the mood of the populace, or the fads of revolutionaries. God's Law is unchanging: "Your righteousness is an everlasting righteousness, / And Your law is truth" (Psa 119:142). "The sum of Your word is truth, / And every one of Your righteous ordinances is everlasting" (Psa 119:160). Therefore, Moses warns God's people: "Whatever I command you, you shall be careful to do; you shall not add to nor take away from it" (Deut 12:32; cp. Psa 119:44, 137, 142, 144).

We must recall that the new covenant does not bring with it a new Law, but rather a new *power* to keep the same Law.

> "Behold, days are coming," declares the Lord, "when I will make a new covenant with the house of Israel and with the house of Judah, not like the covenant which I made with their fathers in the day I took them by the hand to bring them out of the land of Egypt, My covenant which they broke, although I was a husband to them," declares the Lord. "But this is the covenant which I will make with the house of Israel after those days," declares the Lord, "I will put My law within them, and on their heart I will write it; and I will be their God, and they shall be My people." (Jer 31:31–33).

Thus Paul declares in the new covenant era: "Do we then nullify the Law through faith? May it never be! On the contrary, we establish the Law" (Rom 3:31)?

Some decry the law as an imposition of religion. But all law imposes religion in that law is necessarily religious, for all law is an expression of morality. And morality is based on ideas of ultimacy and value. By the very nature of the case ultimacy and values are religious conceptions; they are not mathematical formulas or chemical reactions or physical constructs. The Christian religion, being the truth (as demonstrated by a proper apologetic), provides an inerrant and authoritative Word of unchanging righteousness as the standard of social morality.

2. God's Law promises cultural prosperity. Cultural prosperity abounds due to widespread God-defined righteousness because we live in a moral universe. Scripture teaches the inescapable reality that "the eyes of the Lord are in every place, / Watching the evil and the good" (Prov 15:3; cp. Psa 139:7; Jer 23:24). The God who watches over all things reveals his Law to us in order to define the evil and the good: "I would not have come to know sin except through the Law" (Rom 7:7). We must understand that "righteousness exalts a nation, / But sin is a disgrace to any people" (Prov 14:34).

God is sovereign in his providential administration of world affairs. Consequently, the prophets can poetically portray the clouds as the dust of his feet (Nah 1:3–6). Job can speak of God as directing the lightning (Job 37:3). Jesus says that he even controls the number of hairs on our heads and the life and death of sparrows (Matt 10:29–30). Indeed, He "works *all things* according to the counsel of His will" (Eph 1:11). History has meaning and purpose due to God's personal involvement. Thus, he has ordained that Law obedience determines national destinies in the historical long run.

We see this most clearly expressed in Deuteronomy 28 where God promises personal and social blessings for obedience but threatens cultural and social upheaval for disobedience. The opening section of this chapter promises: "Now it shall be, if you will diligently obey the Lord your God, being careful to do all His commandments which I command you today, the Lord your God will set you high above all the nations of the earth. And all these blessings shall come upon you and overtake you, if you will obey the Lord your God. . . ." (Deut 28:1–2; cf. vv 3–14). And it equally threatens disaster for breach of his Law: "But it shall come about, if you will not obey the Lord your God, to observe to do all His commandments and His statutes with which I charge you today, that all these curses shall come upon you and overtake you" (Deut 28:15; cf. vv 16–68). Other such verses include: Exodus 15:26; 23:22; Leviticus 26: 3–13; Deuteronomy 7:12–26; 11:13–17.

Indeed, Paul expressly teaches that: "Now we know that whatever the Law says, it speaks to those who are under the Law, that every mouth may be closed, and all the world may become accountable to God" (Rom 3:19). Thus, all the world is accountable to God in terms of his Law. His blessings will flow or his curses befall men on the basis of their moral conduct which God evaluates through his Law.

Societal benefits

I will provide a few examples of particular societal benefits that accrue from an approach to culture based on God's Law.

1. God's Law establishes stable monetary policies. It obligates government to maintain just monetary policies by requiring that "you shall not have in your bag differing weights, a large and a small. You shall not have in your house differing measures, a large and a small. You shall have a full and just weight; you shall have a full and just measure, that your days may be prolonged in the land which the Lord your God gives you" (Deut 25:13–15; cp. Lev 19:35–37; Prov 11:1; 20:23; Eze 45:10; Mic 6:11). The Law thereby prohibits three contemporary monetary phenomena that have contributed so heavily to the economically precarious position of modern nations: fiat money, fractional reserve banking, and deficit spending.

2. God's Law provides a moral basis for elective, representative governmental officials. We see the Law establishing elective government in the following passage:

Choose wise and discerning and experienced men from your tribes, and I will appoint them as your heads. . . . So I took the heads of your tribes, wise and experienced men, and appointed them heads over you, leaders of thousands, and of hundreds, of fifties and of tens, and officers for your tribes. . . . You shall not show partiality in judgment; you shall hear the small and the great alike. You shall not fear man, for the judgment is God's. And the case that is too hard for you, you shall bring to me, and I will hear it. (Deut 1:13, 15, 17)

3. God's Law encourages equitable taxation. God forbids undue, abusive taxation of the rich: "The rich shall not pay more, and the poor shall not pay less than the half shekel, when you give the contribution to the Lord to make atonement for yourselves" (Exo 30:15). Socialistic policies punish the wealthy — and the poor — whereas God's Law protects the rights of both the poor and rich.

4. God's Law calls for a system of just restitution. Rather than establishing a prison system the Law warns that :

If a man steals an ox or a sheep, and slaughters it or sells it, he shall pay five oxen for the ox and four sheep for the sheep. If the thief is caught while breaking in, and is struck so that he dies, there will be no blood-guiltiness on his account. But if the sun has risen on him, there will be bloodguiltiness on his account. He shall surely make restitution; if he owns nothing, then he shall be sold for his theft.[1] If what he stole is actually found alive in his possession, whether an ox or a donkey or a sheep, he shall pay double." (Exo 22:1–4, cp. vv 7–9)

Thus, it would justly reimburse crime victims, eliminate taxpayer support of criminals, and rid society of a major training ground for criminals.

5. God's Law insures criminal justice. For instance, the Law forbids the pardoning and paroling of court-convicted murderers by requiring their execution:

But if there is a man who hates his neighbor and lies in wait for him and rises up against him and strikes him so that he dies, and he flees to one of these cities, then the elders of his city shall send and take him from there and deliver him into the hand of the avenger of blood, that he may die. You shall not pity him, but you shall purge the blood of the innocent from Israel, that it may go well with you. (Deut 19:11–13)

Capital punishment is am often repeated theme in God's Law: "He who strikes a man so that he dies shall surely be put to death" (Exo

---

[1] This indentured servitude would force the thief literally to pay for his crime.

21:12). "But if he struck him down with an iron object, so that he died, he is a murderer; the murderer shall surely be put to death" (Num 35:16). The justification for capital punishment arises from the nature of man as the image of God: "Whoever sheds man's blood, / By man his blood shall be shed, / For in the image of God / He made man" (Gen 9:6).

6. *God's Law punishes malicious, frivolous lawsuits.* Rather than allowing and even encouraging a lawyer-based society, God establishes a law-based society. For instance, his Law warns:

> If a malicious witness rises up against a man to accuse him of wrong-doing, then both the men who have the dispute shall stand before the Lord, before the priests and the judges who will be in office in those days. And the judges shall investigate thoroughly; and if the witness is a false witness and he has accused his brother falsely, then you shall do to him just as he had intended to do to his brother. Thus you shall purge the evil from among you. And the rest will hear and be afraid, and will never again do such an evil thing among you. (Deut 19:16–20)

7. *God's Law protects unborn human life.* The Law of God not only does not condone abortion it vigorously legislates against it:

> If men fight, and hurt a woman with child, so that she gives birth prema-turely, yet no harm follows, he shall surely be punished accordingly as the woman's husband imposes on him; and he shall pay as the judges determine. But if any harm follows, then you shall give life for life. (Exo 21:22–23 NKJV)

When this case law states "yet no harm follows," it means no harm to *either* the mother *or* the child. Here we see severe judicial consequences for even an accidental abortion, how much more would this law bear upon intentional abortion. Abortion is not only a sin, but a crime, and, indeed, a capital crime.

Conclusion

Since God governs the Universe and knows all things, he reveals a Law that is applicable to all times. In this chapter I surveyed a few ran-dom illustrations of the practical utility of God's Law. I could present many more samples, but that would expand this book beyond the para-meters of the Made *Easy* Series. For additional, more-detailed information I would recommend the following much larger works.

Stephen C. Halbrook, God Is Just: A Defense of the Old Testament Civil Laws (2d. ed.: Theonomy Resources Media, 2014).

Gary North, Leviticus: *An Economic Commentary* (Tyler, Tex.: Institute for Christian Economics, 1995).

Gary North, *Moses and Pharaoh: Dominion Religion Versus Power Religion* (Tyler, Tex.: Institute for Christian Economics, 1985).

Gary North, *Sinai Strategy: Economics and the Ten Commandments* (Tyler, Tex.: Institute for Christian Economics, 1986),

Gary North, *Tools of Dominion: The Case Laws of Exodus* (Tyler, Tex.: Institute for Christian Economics, 1990).

Rousas J. Rushdoony, *The Institutes of Biblical Law* (Vallecito, Calif.: Ross House, 1973).

Rousas J. Rushdoony, *Law and Society: The Institutes of Biblical Law* (Vallecito, Calif.: Ross House, 1982).

Chapter 8
Historical Confession and God's Law

We have been considering the case for the continuing relevance and application of God's Law in the new covenant era and the modern world. Historically, Reformed theology has been the clearest and most vigorous proponent of God's Law, whereas most other evangelical theologies either overlook it altogether or studiously discount it as a viable option in ethical and legal discourse.

In that we are interested in the historical continuance of the Law even in the field of civil jurisprudence, a brief study of an historical specimen of Reformed theological commitment should prove helpful. In this chapter I will present a study of the historical question as found in the venerable Westminster Confession of Faith, the leading Reformed confession in the world today. This study will be important for demonstrating the historical and theological legitimacy for affirming the Law. Let us see how the Westminster divines strongly endorsed the Law.

Positive Affirmation of God's Law
Before entering into the Confession itself, I will present a few samples from the other writings of the Westminster divines which prove their endorsement of the Law.

Specimens from the Divines
As I begin the reader should bear two points in mind: (1) Where necessary I have updated the seventeenth century style to make it more readable. For example, "he must not punish no sinnes" becomes "he must not punish sins." (2) Some of the citations will assert positions that contemporary proponents of God's Law do not maintain. Nevertheless, these citations are valuable as historical witnesses to a Reformed commitment to the Law in civil ethics. I do not endorse all of the views cited. Not only are the divines not infallible, but we must engage in legitimate debate over the details of application — just as we debate the various features of theology itself.

George Gillespie (1613–48)

One of the leading Westminster divines was Scottish commissioner George Gillespie. He not only voted for the Westminster Confession of Faith, he helped write it. Hetherington claims that Gillespie "became one of the most prominent members of that August assembly, although the youngest man and minister of the whole."[1] In fact, "he took an equally active and influential part in the framing of the Confession of Faith and the Catechisms, which embodied the doctrinal decisions of the Assembly."[2]

In *Wholesome Severity Reconciled with Christian Liberty* Gillespie offers remarkably strong endorsements of the Law, which I shall cite in part, beginning with his second point:

> (2) Christ's words (Matt. 5:17), "Think not that I am come to destroy the Law or the Prophets, I am not come to destroy, but to fulfill," are comprehensive of the judicial law, it being a part of the law of Moses. Now he could not fulfill the judicial law, except either by his practice, or by teaching others still to observe it; not by his own practice, for he would not condemn the adulteress (Jn. 8:11), nor divide the inheritance (Luke 12:13–14). Therefore it must be by his doctrine for our observing it.

> (3) If Christ in his sermon (Matt. 5), would teach that the moral law belongs to us Christians, in so much as he vindicates it from the false glosses of the scribes and Pharisees; then he meant to hold forth the judicial law concerning moral trespasses as belonging unto us also; for he vindicates and interprets the judicial law, as well as the moral (Matt. 5:38), An eye for an eye, etc.

> (4) If God would have the moral law transmitted from the Jewish people to the Christian people; then he would also have the judicial laws transmitted form the Jewish Magistrate to the Christian Magistrate: there being the same reason of immutability in the punishments, which is in the offenses.[3]

---

[1] William Hetherington, *History of the Westminster Assembly of Divines* (Edmonton: Still Waters Revival, rep. 1991 [1856]), 400.

[2] Hetherington, *History of the Westminster Assembly*, 401.

[3] Cited in Christopher Coldwell, ed., *Anthology of Presbyterian & Reformed Literature* (Dallas: Naphtali, 1991), 182–183

Samuel Rutherford (1600–61)

Another of the Scottish divines, Samuel Rutherford, was a theologian of great stature and influence. Hetherington notes of him that: "While he attended that Assembly, he greatly distinguished himself by his skill in debate, his eloquence in preaching, and his great learning and ability as an author. Few works of that age surpass, or even equal, those which were produced by Rutherford, during that intensely laborious period of his life."[4]

Rutherford writes of the civil magistrate in his most important work *Lex, Rex*:

> The execution of their office is an act of the just Lord of heaven and earth, not only by permission, but according to God's revealed will in his word; their judgment is not the judgment of men, but of the Lord, 2 Chron. 19:6, and their throne is the throne of God, 1 Chron. 22:10. Jerome saith, to punish murderers and sacrilegious persons is not bloodshed, but the ministry and service of good laws. So, if the king be a living law by office, and the law put in execution which God hath commanded, then, as the moral law is by divine institution, so must the officer of God be, who is *custos et vindex legis divnae*, the keeper, preserver, and avenger of God's law.[5]

Later he observes in a similar vein (44:16):

> As the king is under God's law both in commanding and in exacting active obedience, so is he under the same regulating law of God, in punishing or demanding of us passive subjection, and as he may not command what he will, but what the King of kings warranteth him to command, so may he not punish as he will, but by warrant also of the Supreme Judge of all the earth.[6]

In another work titled *The Due Right of Presbyteries, or, a Peaceable Plea*, Rutherford writes:

> It is clear the question must be thus stated, for all the laws of the Old Testament (which we hold in their Moral equity to be perpetual) that are touching blasphemies, heresies, solicitation to worship false Gods and the breach of which the Godly Magistrate was to punish, command or forbid only such things as may be proved by two or three witnesses, and which *husband and*

---

[4] Hetherington, *History of the Westminster Assembly*, 394.

[5] Samuel Rutherford, *Lex, Rex, or The Law and the Prince* (Harrisonburg, Vir.,: Sprinkle, rep. 1982 [1644]), 4.

[6] Rutherford, *Lex Rex*, 232.

wife are not to conceal, and from which all *Israel* must abstain for fear of the like punishment. Deut. 13:8, 9, 10, 11; Deut. 17:5, 6; Lev. 20:1, 2, 3, 4. But opinions in the mind, acts of the understanding, can never be proved by witnesses and such as neither *Magistrates* nor *Church* can censure.[7]

Other Divines

Jeremiah Burroughs (1599–1646). Speaking of a capital sanctions text considered an embarrassment to advocates of God's Law today, Burroughs commented on Deuteronomy 13:

> Let not any put off this Scripture, saying, This is in the Old Testament but we find no such thing in the gospel, for we find the same thing almost the same words used in a prophecy of the times of the gospel (Zech. 13:3). [Of Zech. 13 he observed:] You must understand this by that in Deuteronomy. The meaning is not that his father or mother should presently run a knife into him, but that though they begat him, yet they should be the means to bring him to condign punishment, even the taking away of his life; those who were the instruments of his life, should now be the instruments of his death.[8]

Herbert Palmer (1601–1647). Palmer argued from a methodology employing God's Law, noting that

> this general rule gives me leave to assert and commend to your most serious considerations and consciences: That whatsoever Law of God, or command of His, we find recorded in the Law-book, in either of the volumes of God's statute, the New Testament or the Old Testament, remains obligatory to us, unless we can prove it to be expired, or repealed. So it is with the statute-law of this nation, or of any nation.[9]

William Reyner (d. 1666). In referring to the capital sanctions against idolatry, Reyner argued: "This duty is principally incumbent upon the magistrate, who is to execute judgment of the Lord, not arbitrarily as he himself pleaseth; but according to the rule of the Word, both for matter and manner."[10]

---

[7] Samuel Rutherford, *The Due Right of Presbyteries, or, A Peaceable Please* (London: 1644), 358.

[8] Jeremiah Burroughs, *Irenicum, to the Lovers of Truth and Peace* (London: 1646), 19-20.

[9] Herbert Palmer, *The Glasse of God's Providence Towards His Faithfull Ones*. Sermon before Parliament (Aug. 13, 1644), 52.

[10] William Reyner, *Babylons Ruining: Earthquake and the Restoration of Zion*. A sermon preached before the House of Commons, August 28, 1644.

Richard Vines (1600–1655). Vines vigorously argued for the continuance of capital sanctions against blasphemers:

> For the blasphemous and seditious heretics, both Lutherans and others
> of the Reformed churches do agree that they may be punished capitally,
> that is for their blasphemy or sedition. But the Socinian stands out here
> also, and denies it, alleging that the punishment of false prophets in that
> was *especiali jure* by special law granted to the *Israelites*, and therefore
> you must not look (saith the Socinian) into the Old Testament for a rule
> of proceeding against false prophets and blasphemers: Nor (saith *Calvin*
> and *Catharinus*) can you find in the New Testament any precept for the
> punishment of thieves, traitors, adulterers, witches, murders and the
> like, and yet they may, or at least some of them may be capitally pun-
> ished: for the gospel destroys not the just laws of civil policy or com-
> monwealths.[11]

Explanations from the Confession

I will now consider a passage within the Westminister Confession
that seems to contradict the views of the divines cited above. This passage is widely misunderstood in the debate over God's Law. I am speaking about the statement in 19:4:

> WCF 19:4: To them also, as a body politic, He gave sundry judicial laws,
> which expired together with the State of that people; not obliging any
> other now, further than the general equity thereof may require.

A cursory reading of WCF 19:4 sounds contrary to the continuing
relevance of the judicial law. Does it not declare the judicial laws "expired"? Are we not informed that they are "not obliging any other now"?
Does it not reduce the concrete judicial laws to a vague "general equity"?
This certainly appears contradictory to what I have been arguing, but
looks are deceiving.

Historical presumption

Just as we must understand the *occasional* nature of the New Testament epistles if we are to more properly understand and more deeply
appreciate them,[12] so must we understand the historical setting of the

---

[11] Richard Vines, *The Authours, Nature and Danger of Haeresie. Laid Open in a
Sermon Preached before the Honourable House of Commons* (London: 1647), 64.

[12] George W. Knight, III, "The Scriptures Were Written for Our Instruction,"
in *Journal of the Evangelical Theological Society*, 39 (March, 1996): 3–14.

Westminster Assembly if we are to grasp the reasoning of the divines. We are all children of our times; we all speak from our historical contexts. And so it is in the Westminster Standards: they were not alien intrusions into a placid life of political indifference. In fact, the calling of the Assembly itself was fraught with political significance and urged on the basis of political pressures.

The Early Reformers. First, the endorsement of God's Law was clearly established among the early Reformers. Calvin's Geneva — though neither perfect nor wholly consistent — rightly serves as an experimental model of the role of God's Law in political theory and practice.[13] Calvin had strong predilections toward the application of the Law to contemporary socio-political matters.

In his commentary on the much maligned thirteenth chapter of Deuteronomy, *John Calvin* (1509–64) noted: "Whoever shall now contend that it is unjust to put heretics and blasphemers to death will knowingly and willingly incur their very guilt. This is not laid down on human authority; it is God who speaks and prescribes a perpetual rule for his Church." He even scathingly criticizes those who would oppose his position: "Some scoundrel or other gainsays this, and sets himself against the author of life and death. What insolence is this. . . . God has pronounced what is His will, for we must needs abide by His inviolable decree."[14]

As Philip Schaff notes: "Calvin's plea for the right and duty of the Christian magistrate to punish heresy by death, stands or falls with his theocratic theory and the binding authority of the Mosaic code. His arguments are chiefly drawn from the Jewish laws against idolatry and blasphemy, and from the examples of the pious kings of Israel."[15]

Martin Bucer (1491–1551), an enormous influence on Calvin, argued:

> But since no one can describe an approach more equitable and wholesome to the commonwealth than that which God describes in His law, it is certainly the duty of all kings and princes who recognize that God

---

[13] See: Jack W. Sawyer, Jr., "Moses and the Magistrate: Aspects of Calvin's Political Theory in Contemporary Focus" (Master's Thesis: Westminster Theological Seminary, 1986).

[14] John Calvin, *Commentaries on the Four Last Books of Moses* (Grand Rapids: Baker, rep. 1979), 3:78.

[15] Philip Schaff, *History of the Christian Church,* vol. 8 (3d. ed.: Grand Rapids: Eerdmans, rep. n.d. [1910]), 792.

has put them over His people that they follow most studiously His own method of punishing evildoers.[16]

Bucer immediately annexes to this statement a list of capital crimes from the Mosaic legislation, and then notes a little later that the king must "for every single crime" impose "those penalties which the Lord Himself has sanctioned."[17]

John Knox (1514–72) commented on Deuteronomy 17 as follows. Please note again: my understanding of this passage differs from his. Nevertheless, we must recognize his clear presumption of the authoritative and binding applicability of God's Law:

> If any thinks that the fore written law did bind the Jews only, let the same man consider that the election of a king and appointing of judges did neither appertain to the ceremonial law, neither yet was it merely judicial; but that it did flow from the moral law, as an ordinance having respect to the conservation of both the tables. . . . [Consequently] it is evident, that the office of the king or supreme magistrate, has respect to the moral law, and to the conservation of both tables.[18]

Swiss Reformer and successor to Ulrich Zwingli, *Johann Heinrich Bullinger* (1504–1575) wrote that "the substance of God's judicial laws is not taken away or abolished, but the ordering and imitation of them is placed in the arbitrement of good Christian princes." In chapter 30 on the Civil Magistrate Bullinger wrote of the civil ruler:

> Let him govern the people, committed to him of God, with good laws, made according to the Word of God in his hands, and look that nothing be taught contrary thereunto. . . . Therefore let him draw forth this sword of God against all malefactors, seditious persons, thieves, murderers, oppressors, blasphemers, perjured persons, and all those whom God has commanded him to punish or even to execute.

Thus, we discover in these influential Reformers a clear pattern of inclination toward God's Law in socio-political theory. These are deep tributaries feeding the Puritan stream of thought.

---

[16] Martin Bucer, *De Regno Christi*, trans. and ed. by Wilhelm Pauck, *The Library of Christian Classics*, vol. 19 (Philadelphia: Westminster, 1954), 378.

[17] Bucer, *De Regno Christi*, 383.

[18] John Knox, "The First Blast of the Trumpet against the Monstrous Regiment of Women," in *Selected Writings of John Knox* (Dallas: Presbyterian Heritage, 1995), 408.

Westminster Contemporaries. Second, the contemporary Reformed influence beyond the Westminster Assembly clearly adopted a conviction regarding the binding obligation of God's judicial laws in the civil sphere. Here I have space only for a few samples from the wider Puritan community.

Prominent Massachusetts Bay pastor *John Cotton* (1584–1652) published an influential work which became the foundation of the civil code of Massachusetts: *An Abstract of the Laws of New England, as They are Now Established.* This work and the civil code based upon it quote extensively from the Mosaic code.

Another Massachusetts Puritan, *Thomas Shepard* (1605–1649) argues that "the judicial laws, some of them being hedges and fences to safeguard both moral and ceremonial precepts, their binding power was therefore mixed and various, for those which did safeguard any moral law, (which is perpetual,) whether by just punishments or otherwise, do still morally bind all nations." He continued by noting: "God would have all nations preserve their fences forever, as he would have that law preserved forever which these safeguard."[19]

James Durham (1622–1658) distinguishes between the three categories of law and notes that "the judicial law is for regulating outward society, and for government, and doth generally (excepting what was peculiar to the people of Israel) agree with the moral law."[20] Durham classes the capital sanction for adultery in the "moral" category when he observes that adultery "is a heinous crime worthy to be punished by the judge. The laws of man should take order with such a sin, and the moral law of God taught that such a sin deserved death (Deut. 22:22), not only in the woman, as some would have it only, but also in the man."[21]

The Records of the New Haven Colony (1641–1644) presents the following endorsement of God's judicial law:

> The judicial law of God given by Moses and expounded in other parts of scripture, so far as it is a hedge and a fence to the moral laws, and neither ceremonial nor typical nor had any reference to Canaan, hath an everlasting *equity* it, and should be the rule of our proceedings . . . . It

---

[19] Thomas Shepard, *The Morality of the Sabbath* in *The Works of Thomas Shepard*, vol. 3, (Boston: Doctrinal Tract and Book Society, 1853), 53ff.

[20] James Durham, *The Law Unsealed; or, a Practical Exposition of the Ten Commandments* (Glasgow: 1798), 22.

[21] James Durham, *Lectures on Job* (Dallas: Naphtali, 1995), 170.

was ordered that the judicial laws of God, as they were delivered by Moses . . . be a rule to all the courts in this jurisdiction in their proceedings against offenders.

Third, as I show above the Westminster divines themselves display a marked propensity to applying God's Law in political ethics.

After all this historical research is sorted and analyzed, how can the Westminster Standards be opposed to the contemporary application of the judicial laws? Is not their Reformational history conducive to such? Do not their framers frequently apply Mosaic penalties in judicial contexts? Do they not vigorously argue for the continuing validity of the Mosaic sanctions?

Philosophical complexion

In light of all the historical and literary evidence for the Puritans' application of the Mosaic judicial laws to contemporary political matters, we should not be surprised that the Standards share this same family complexion. This is true even in the 1788 Americanized edition of the Confession, but is especially obvious in the original documents adopted by the Westminster Assembly. I will summarize the legal tendencies of confessional political philosophy under two heads.

Westminster and the Civil Magistrate. First, the Confession's chapter on the civil magistrate clearly inclines toward a political philosophy governed by God's Law. This is most clearly delineated in WCF 23:1:

God, the supreme Lord and King of all the world, has ordained civil magistrates, to be, under Him, over the people, for His own glory, and the public good: and, to this end, has armed them with the power of the sword, for the defence and encouragement of them that are good, and for the punishment of evil doers.

Thus, the Westminster socio-political philosophy asserts that:

1. God positively ordains civil authority. Here we have — quite in keeping with the full-orbed Calvinistic theology of the Confession elsewhere, although not all that controversial — the declaration that the civil magistracy is positively established by God. Civil rule is not merely an evolutionary sociological happenstance; nor is it an aspect of man's ethical rebellion against God; nor is it a matter of indifference to God. The Lord positively ordains civil rule over men gathered in societies, so that to resist civil authority in its "lawful power, or the lawful exercise of it" is to "resist the ordinance of God" (WCF 20:4).

In fact, here we learn that the divines held that the civil magistrate may "lawfully" punish men for:

> publishing of such opinions, or maintaining of such practices, as are contrary to the light of nature, or to the *known principles of Christianity* (whether concerning faith, worship, or conversation), or to the power of godliness; or, such erroneous opinions or practices, as either in their own nature, or in the manner of publishing or maintaining them, are destructive to the external peace and order which Christ has established in the Church, they may lawfully be called to account, and proceeded against, by the censures of the Church *and by the power of the civil magistrate* (20: 4b).[22]

2. God sovereignly limits (i.e., morally constrains) civil authority. In addition to the previous observation which is rather widely accepted, we find a phrase more narrowly conceived: the magistrate is "to be under Him" (23:1a). "God, the supreme Lord and King of all the world, has ordained civil magistrates, to be, under Him."

Here the Confession rebukes the then-current notion of the divine right of kings by stating that even the king is *under* God. Consequently, he is deemed a servant of God and morally bound to recognize his own servant position in the world, that is, *under God* though *over the people.* Larger Catechism 124 designates magistrates as "superiors" ordained by God to be obeyed: "By father and mother, in the fifth commandment, are meant, not only natural parents, but *all superiors* in age and gifts; and *especially such as, by God's ordinance, are over us in place of authority*, whether in family, church, or *commonwealth.*"

The civil magistrate is a "superior" who must govern *lawfully*, that is, according to God's Law. Thus, the Westminster Larger Catechism 127 reads:

> The honor which inferiors owe to their superiors is, all due reverence in heart, word, and behavior; prayer and thanksgiving for them; imitation of their virtues and graces; willing obedience to their *lawful commands* and counsels; due submission to their corrections; fidelity to, defense and maintenance of their persons and authority, according to their several ranks, and the nature of their places; bearing with their infirmities, and covering them in love, that so they may be an honor to them and to their government.

---

[22] The italicized portion both emphasizes the important phrase and highlights the American deletion from the Confession.

One Confessional illustration of "lawful" civil authority is the keeping and promoting of the sabbath, which is obviously an element in God's Law:

> The charge of keeping the sabbath is more specially directed to governors of families, and *other superiors*, because they are bound not only to keep it themselves, *but to see that it be observed by all those that are under their charge*; and because they are prone ofttimes to hinder them by employments of their own" (LC 118).

Another illustration is the Confession's disallowing incestuous relations *as defined in God's Law*:

> Nor can such incestuous marriages ever be made lawful by any law of man or consent of parties, so as those persons may live together as man and wife. [The man may not marry any of his wife's kindred, nearer in blood then he may of his own: nor the woman of her husband's kindred, nearer in blood than of her own]" (WCF 24:1; cp. LC 139).[23]

The word "lawful" in the context of the Standards refers to those things *allowed by express revelation in God's Word*.

Westminster Proof-texts. Second, the Westminster Standards freely cite from Old Testament judicial laws to justify their creedal stance. If those laws were wholly abrogated, their employment would be futile.

In WCF 20:4 the divines warn of speaking against the "known principles of Christianity"; such would subject one to the threat of punishment by "the civil magistrate." The justification for such, as we see often from their other writings, is the infamous capital sanction against idolatry, Deuteronomy 13. Not only is this judicial law their first proof-text, but they employ others enforcing the Sabbath (Neh 13:15–25) and paralleling the Deuteronomy passage (Zech 13:2–3).

In WCF 22:3 oaths and vows are governed by Numbers 5:12, 19, 21. Civil suppression of "blasphemies and heresies" in WCF 23:3 is proven by referring to capital sanctions in Leviticus 24:16 and Deuteronomy 13:5. Laws forbidding biblically-defined consanguinity are cited in WCF 24:4: Leviticus 18 and 20:19–21. Divorce legislation in WCF 26 is justified by Deuteronomy 24:1–4. False religion must be removed by the civil magistrate, for God requires such in Deuteronomy 7:5 (LC 108) and Deuteronomy 13:6–12 (LC 109). Capital punishment is morally justified in LC 136 by citing Numbers 35:16–21, 31 and Exodus 21:18–36. The capital sanc-

---

[23] Bracketed sentence omitted in American version.

tion against bestiality is appended to LC 139: Leviticus 20:15–16. Restitution is required for theft in LC 141, as required by Leviticus 6:2–5.

Interestingly, Deuteronomy 13 is cited several times in the Standards: WCF 20:4; 23:3; LC 109; and LC 145. In addition, a perusal of Stephen Pribble's helpful *Scripture Index to the Westminster Standards* provides evidence of scores of references to the Mosaic judicial legislation.[24]

Negative Concerns Regarding God's Law

Now let us consider objections to God's Law that some see embodied in WCF 19:4. What are we to make of the Confession's express statements regarding the judicial laws? What do the divines mean when they state:

> To them [the Jews] also, as a body politic, He gave sundry judicial laws, which expired together with the State of that people; not obliging any other now, further than the general equity thereof may require. (WCF 19:4)

Ceremonial abrogation

First, we should note that the divines treat the judicial laws in a fundamentally different way than the ceremonial laws. This observation, though not conclusive, will put us on the right track for discovering their intent.

When we compare the statement in WCF 19:3 on the ceremonial law with 19:4 on the judicial law, we discover a much stronger word used in removing our obligation to the ceremonial: "*All* which ceremonial laws are now *abrogated*, under the New Testament." According to the *Oxford English Dictionary*, the word "abrogated" means "abolished by authority, annulled." Indeed, the word "abrogate" is derived from Latin legal language, being a compound of *ab* ("away") and *rogare* ("to propose a law").

Thus, the Confession states that "all" of these ceremonial laws are positively "abrogated," as by decree, i.e., the revelation of "the New Testament." The statement on the judicial law, to which I will return shortly, is milder: "He gave sundry judicial laws, which *expired*." Neither is it attached to the arrival of the "New Testament."

In WCF 7:5 we read of the nature of the Old Testament economy which is now defunct:

---

[24] Stephen Pribble, *Scripture Index to the Westminster Standards* (Dallas: Presbyterian Heritage, 1994), 9–13.

> This covenant was differently administered in the time of the law, and in the time of the Gospel: under the law it was administered by promises, prophecies, sacrifices, circumcision, the paschal lamb, and other types and ordinances delivered to the people of the Jews, all foresignifying Christ to come; which were, for that time, sufficient and efficacious, through the operation of the Spirit, to instruct and build up the elect in faith in the promised Messiah, by whom they had full remission of sins, and eternal salvation; and is called the Old Testament.

Note that the Old Testament economy was "differently administered in the time of the law." But the positive difference of that administration — which characterizes the oldness of the Old Testament — is defined in terms of *ceremonies* "all foresignifying Christ to come" which refer to the "full remission of sins, and eternal salvation." The Old Testament economy, then, is different, not in regard to its moral character or judicial makeup, but rather in its "types . . . foresignifying Christ." Nothing is said of the judicial law as an aspect of the difference in the new administration. As 19:3 says: the ceremonial law is "abrogated under the New Testament," which is precisely — and *only* — what we see here in WCF 7.

When the New Testament which "abrogates" the Old Testament finally arrives, its difference lies in its conclusive character, as opposed to the typical character of the Old. WCF 7:6 reads:

> Under the Gospel, when Christ, the substance, was exhibited, the ordinances in which this covenant is dispensed are the preaching of the Word, and the administration of the sacraments of Baptism and the Lord's Supper: which, though fewer in number, and administered with more simplicity, and less outward glory, yet, in them, it is held forth in more fullness, evidence, and spiritual efficacy, to all nations, both Jews and Gentiles; and is called the New Testament. There are not therefore two covenants of grace, differing in substance, but one and the same, under various dispensations.

Here the Confession once again fails to describe the covenantal difference of the New Testament by referring to judicial stipulations or civil ethics. In fact, this anti-ceremonial theme, along with a silence regarding judicial matters, continues in WCF 20. There in section 1 we read that "under the New Testament, the liberty of Christians is further enlarged, *in their freedom from the yoke of the ceremonial law,* to which the Jewish Church was subjected." Again: the focal difference is on the *ceremonial*, not the judicial law. Our liberty does not involve a liberty from the judicial law, but from the ceremonial. All of this will become more evident below.

Judicial expiration

Second, in WCF 19:4 the milder term "expired" implies inherent elements in the judicial laws that simply fail to function any longer. They are not positively "abrogated"; they are not judicially repealed. If the same result befalls both the judicial and the ceremonial laws, as those opposed to God's Law declare, why were the judicial laws not declared "abrogated," then reference made to the New Testament for judicial principles? The Confession, after all, has a clear concern for political and judicial ethics. And why do the judicial laws appear frequently in the proof-texts for the Larger Catechism exposition of the Ten Commandments? These are inexplicable on the position of those opposed to God's Law.

Admittedly, the Confession does note that the judicial laws "expired." That is, they expired along with the Jewish "State," the "body politic." A hermeneutically sound exegesis of WCF 19:4 must recognize that the expiring of the judicial laws *in the context* refers to their association with the particular "State" of Israel: the laws as *literally expressed* were given to a specific, historically defined "body politic." The very nature of case law is to provide *sample,* concrete illustrations of legally chargeable offenses for a particular culture and time. Case laws do not enumerate each and every possible conceivable criminal infraction.

Consequently, were the Mosaic judicial laws to continue in toto, then we would be morally obligated to build fences around our roofs, use stoning as the method of capital punishment, provide three cities of refuge, punish certain ceremonial infractions, and so forth. Neither the Puritans, nor the Confession, nor modern advocates of God's Law argue for such. The Israel-related, time-bound literal expression of the case laws "expired," because the specific "State" within which they derived their sense expired.

That this statement in the Confession is not functionally equivalent to a wholesale abrogation, as in the case of the ceremonial laws, is evident in the divines' choice of a conceptually different term: "expired," rather than "abrogated." We also see a difference in the proviso added: "not obliging any other now, further than the general equity thereof may require." Clearly, the "general equity" continues from the judicial law, though no such equity continues from the ceremonial law. In fact, one of the proof-texts for this section on the continuing general equity is Matthew 5:17: "Do not think that I came to abolish the Law or the Prophets; I did not come to abolish, but to fulfill." Obviously the divines did not equate "expired" with "abolish" (Matt 5:17) or "abrogated" (WCF 19:3).

Elsewhere we read in WCF 6:6 that *"every* sin, both original and actual, being a transgression of the righteous law of God, and contrary thereunto, does in its own nature, bring guilt upon the sinner, whereby he is bound over to the wrath of God, and curse of the law, and so made subject to death, with *all* miseries spiritual, *temporal*, and eternal." In 19:6 we read: "the threatenings of [the law] serve to show what even their *sins deserve*; and *what afflictions, in this life, they may expect* for them, although freed from the curse thereof threatened in the law." Consequently, the Confession fences in and defends the moral law by allowing the continuance of *"all* . . . temporal" consequences of breaching it. That these "temporal" consequences include temporal sanctions imposed by the civil magistrate is obvious in that "God, the supreme Lord and King of all the world, has ordained civil magistrates, to be, under Him" and "for the punishment of evil doers" (WCF 23:1).

Thus, the divines allow revealed, temporal, judicial responses to guide the magistrate in the New Testament era. The Confession clearly declares this in the original version of WCF 23:3, where we read of one of the civil magistrates' duties that "all blasphemies and heresies be suppressed." Here the divines cited Leviticus 24:16 and Deuteronomy 13:5 as proof-texts. Obviously, an "expired" law still "requiring" a "general equity" is fundamentally different from an "abrogated" law (as per the ceremonial laws).

Furthermore, in Larger Catechism 108 we read the obligation that devolves upon men "according to each one's place and calling":

> The duties required in the second commandment are, the receiving, observing, and keeping pure and entire, all such religious worship and ordinances as God has instituted in his Word; particularly prayer and thanksgiving in the name of Christ; the reading, preaching, and hearing of the Word; the administration and receiving of the sacraments; church government and discipline; the ministry and maintenance thereof; religious fasting; swearing by the name of God, and vowing unto him: as also the disapproving, detesting, opposing, all false worship; and, *according to each one's place and calling, removing it, and all monuments of idolatry.*

The confessional view of "calling" includes the civil magistrate in his public duties: "It is lawful for Christians to accept and execute the office of a magistrate, when *called* thereunto" (WCF 23:2). Thus, of the second commandment, Larger Catechism 108 directs the civil ruler to oppose and remove all monuments of idolatry — *as required in various judicial laws of the Old Testament.* The proof-texts cited include Deuteronomy 7:5, a judicial case law. The next question, a follow-up to Larger Catechism 108, also cites Deuteronomy 13:6–8.

Larger Catechism 99, speaking on the fundamental moral law contained in the Ten Commandments, agrees:

> That what is forbidden or commanded to ourselves, we are bound, *according to our places*, to endeavor that it may be avoided or performed by others, *according to the duty of their places*. That in what is commanded to others, we are bound, *according to our places and callings*, to be helpful to them; and to take heed of partaking with others in what is forbidden them.

As noted previously, the unedited original of WCF 23:3 says of the magistrate that "he has *authority*, and it is his *duty*, to take order that unity and peace be preserved in the Church, that the truth of God be kept pure and entire, that *all blasphemies and heresies be suppressed*." Here again the divines refer to Deuteronomy 13 in their proof-texts. Though the modern argument for God's Law might not urge this response to theological heresy, who can assert that the Confession has wholly removed the judicial laws from consideration?

Equity continuation

Third, the exclusionary clause in WCF 19:4 reminds us that though the judicial laws have "expired," their "general equity" has not. Indeed, their equity will "require" (not: "suggest" or "encourage" or "allow") application: "To them also, as a body politic, He gave sundry judicial laws, which expired together with the State of that people; not obliging any other now, further than the *general equity* thereof may *require*." Here we must determine the meaning of the phrase "general equity" in its historical and Confessional context.

According to the OED the term "equity," when applied to matters of legal jurisprudence, speaks of the "recourse to general principles of justice . . . to correct or supplement the provisions of the law." The "equity of a statute," therefore, involves "the construction of a statue according to its reason and spirit, so as to make it apply to cases for which it does not expressly provide." Obviously the divines would not assert that we need "to correct" God's Law, for it is his very word (WCF 1:4).

Consequently, the remaining "equity" must speak of the underlying principles, the "reason and spirit" of the Law when we "make it apply to cases for which it does not expressly provide." Thus, in their view the Law's equity extends to modern situations (it is still binding; it is "required"), even though the particular ancient and ceremonially-dominated features of Israel no longer exist (it "expired" because given to a specific "body politic").

Perhaps one of the best tools for understanding the Confession at this point is Scripture itself — particularly the King James Version. The Assembly wrote the Confession of Faith in Elizabethan English identical with the KJV, even employing its phraseology and using it as the text for the Scripture proof-texts. As Donald Remillard notes in his *A Contemporary Edition of the Westminster Confession of Faith*: "The initial text of the Westminster Confession of Faith was presented to the English speaking people in 1646. This occurred only thirty-five years after the publication of the King James version of the Bible in 1611. Consequently, its original grammar and vocabulary reflect a mode of communication long dated and 'foreign' to contemporary forms and styles of English usage."[25] We may reasonably conclude that the term "equity" in WCF 19:4 would have the same linguistic function as that in the KJV, which the Confession reflects.

The word "equity" appears numerous times in the KJV, several of which show that God's Law is the standard of equitable righteousness and of sure justice. Psalm 98:9b reads: "with righteousness shall he judge the world, and the people with *equity*." Notice the parallel of "righteousness" and "*equity*." God's Law is inherently and necessarily righteous, as Deuteronomy 4:8 informs us: "What great nation is there that has statutes and judgments as righteous as this whole law which I am setting before you today?"

Following the Mosaic pattern here in Deuteronomy 4, God's righteousness is frequently paralleled with God's Law in Scripture (Isa 42:21; 51:7; Hab 1:4; Rom 3:21; 7:12). In fact, Psalm 119 *frequently* parallels God's law, statutes, ordinances with "righteousness" (Psa 119:7, 40, 62, 75, 106, 121, 123, 137–138, 142, 144, 160, 164, 172)

Psalm 99:4 states that "the king's strength also loveth judgment; thou dost establish *equity*, thou executest judgment and righteousness in Jacob." Notice the parallel of *equity* with the king's judgment and righteousness. Proverbs 1:3 urges us "to receive the instruction of wisdom, justice, and judgment, and *equity*." Here we must note the inclusion of *equity* with wisdom, justice and judgment. Proverbs 2:9 follows suit when

---

[25] Donald Remillard, *Contemporary Edition of the Westminster Confession of Faith* (Ligonier, Penn.: Presby Press, 1988), v.

it observes: "Then shalt thou understand righteousness, and judgment, and *equity*; yea, every good path."

Isaiah 11:4a prophesies that "with righteousness shall he judge the poor, and reprove with *equity* for the meek of the earth." Isaiah 59:14 laments that "judgment is turned away backward, and justice standeth afar off: for truth is fallen in the street, and *equity* cannot enter." Micah 3:9 rebukes Israel: "Hear this, I pray you, ye heads of the house of Jacob, and princes of the house of Israel, that abhor judgment, and pervert all *equity*."

This concept of the continuing, obligatory equity of God's Law was common among the Puritans in the era of the Westminster Assembly. According to historian Thomas Hutchinson, Thomas Cartwright "who had a chief hand in reducing puritanism to a system, held, that the magistrate was bound to adhere to the judicial law of Moses, and might not punish or pardon otherwise than they prescribed."[26] Yet in 1575 Cartwright observed, in keeping with both the Confessional equity approach to law, observed:

> And, as for the judicial law, forasmuch as there are some of them made in regard of the region where they were given, and of the people to whom they were given, the prince and magistrate, keeping the substance and *equity* of them (as it were the marrow), may change the circumstance of them, as the times and places and manners of the people shall require. But to say that any magistrate can save the life of blasphemers, contemptuous and stubborn idolaters, murderers, adulterers, incestuous persons, and such like, which God by his judicial law hath commanded to be put to death, I do utterly deny, and am ready to prove, if that pertained to this question.[27]

Puritan William Perkins concurred with Cartwright's approach when he wrote around 1600: "The witch truly convicted is to be punished with death, the highest degree of punishment, and that by the law of Moses, the *equity* whereof is perpetual."[28] Philip Stubbs (d. 1610), an influential Puritan and author of *An Anatomie of Abuses* asked: "What kind of punish-

---

[26] Thomas Hutchinson, *The History of the Colony and Province of Massachusetts Bay*, ed., Lawrence S. Mayo (New York: Kraus, rep. 1970 [1864]), 2:354.

[27] From Thomas Cartwright's *Second Reply*, cited in *Works of John Whitgift* (Parker Society ed., Cambridge: University Press, 1851), 1:270.

[28] Cited in Rossell H. Robbins, *Encyclopedia of Witchcraft and Demonology* (New York: Crown, 1959), 382.

ment would you have appointed for these notorious bloody swearers? I would wish (if it pleased God) that it were made death: For we read in the law of God, that whosoever blasphemeth the Lord, was presently stoned to death without all remorce. Which law *judicial* standeth in force to the world's end."[29]

From these sample Puritans — Perkins, Cartwright, and Stubbs — the binding character of God's Law lies not in its ancient, Israel-based form (by stoning, after fleeing to cities of refuge, and upon consulting elders in the gates). Nevertheless, in the cases involving capital crimes, the underlying equity continues to require death even in the new covenant era.

Consider the famed Puritan scholar John Owen's thoughts:

> Although the institutions and examples of the Old Testament, of the duty of magistrates in the things and about the worship of God, are not, in their whole latitude and extent, to be drawn into rules that should be obligatory to all magistrates now. . . , yet, doubtless, there is something moral in those institutions, which, being unclothed of their Judaical form, is still binding to all in the like kind, as to some analogy and proportion. Subduct from those administrations what was proper to, and lies upon the account of, the church and nation of the Jews, and what remains upon the general notion of a church and nation must be everlastingly binding.[30]

The modern advocate of God's Law would agree that that which is "expired" in the judicial laws are those literal elements structuring it for Israel as a nation: the particular land arrangements which allowed for cities of refuge, blood avengers, elders in the gates, stoning, levirate marriages, and the like. Or those constructions applying to the peculiar ancient circumstances, the accidental historical and cultural factors of Israel: fences around rooftops, goring oxen, flying axheads, and so forth. The Westminster Standards are clearly sympathetic to the modern application of God's Law.

---

[29] Philip Stubbs, *An Anatomie of Abuses* (1583), as cited in Thomas Rogers, *Exposition of the Thirty-nine Articles* (Cambridge: University Press, 1854), 90.

[30] John Owen, *The Works of John Owen* (London: Banner of Truth, rep. 1967), 8:394.

Conclusion

Though too many evangelical Christians reject God's Law today, we have seen in this chapter that Reformed theology has strongly endorsed it. In fact, some prominent strands of Reformed thought have vigorously promoted even the judicial laws. Thus, our argument for God's Law is not a peculiar approach to the matter. Rather it has a strong influence in Christianity's strongest theological system: Reformed theology.

I would remind the reader that I do not endorse all the conclusions of the authors cited above. Some of them, I believe, went too far. Nevertheless, their witness does show that some branches of evangelical theology have adopted God's Law as the ultimate reference point not only for general ethics, but even for civil jurisprudence.

Chapter 9

CONCLUSION

Despite much confusion from detractors of God's Law, modern advocates of his holy Law are not employing it as a plan for works-justification. We simply teach that the Word of God is the supreme standard by which all men will be judged. That standard is a revealed and objective criterion that takes the guesswork out of righteous living.

Neither does modern application of the Law involve an attempt to force Christianity on a nation by raw political, judicial, or martial imposition. Certainly the standard provided by God's Law is a pattern for all of life, not just the inner-personal sphere of human existence. But the long-range implementation of God's Law must follow, not precede, massive Christian revival. Then, a nation of judicially righteous people will seek a judicially righteous government, according to the standard of God's righteousness, not fallen and sinful man's.

In the final analysis, the alert Christian must understand that the only alternative to God's Law is man's Law. There is no neutrality. This is a fundamental principle of Christian truth. For instance, Jesus said "he who is not with Me is against Me" (Luke 11:23a) and "no servant can serve two masters; for either he will hate the one and love the other, or else he will be loyal to the one and despise the other" (Luke 16:13a). The Bible nowhere disestablishes God's Law, in fact it everywhere affirms it. We should expect that God's Law continues into the New Testament era, unless God himself speaks in Scripture to annuls it, either overtly in direct precept or implicitly in apostolic practice.

Whether God's Law is congenial to our personal feelings or our contemporary environment is not the issue for the Christian. That it is the binding and obligatory standard of God's justice is the sole issue that should concern us.

Christianity has given birth to the greatest prosperity, stability, and liberty known in history. To the extent that the Christian view is also the biblical view (contrary to liberalism, which attempts to separate the two[1]), we may expect God's objective blessings upon that people whose God is the Lord, as evidenced in their law code.

The Christianity of the Bible provides a life-encompassing worldview. True Christianity has an authoritative word from God for all of life.

- So keep and do them, for that is your wisdom and your understanding in the sight of the peoples who will hear all these statutes and say, "Surely this great nation is a wise and understanding people." For what great nation is there that has a god so near to it as is the Lord our God whenever we call on Him? Or what great nation is there that has statutes and judgments as righteous as this whole law which I am setting before you today? (Deut 4:6–8)
- We know that the Law is good, if one uses it lawfully, realizing the fact that law is not made for a righteous man, but for those who are lawless and rebellious, for the ungodly and sinners, for the unholy and profane, for those who kill their fathers or mothers, for murderers and immoral men and homosexuals and kidnappers and liars and perjurers, and whatever else is contrary to sound teaching, according to the glorious gospel of the blessed God, with which I have been entrusted. (1 Tim 1:8–11)

---

[1] In defense of the Presbyterian Church, USA special report on human sexuality in 1991, John Carey, chairman of the committee that wrote the report, commented: "Biblical ethics and Christian ethics for the church today are not the same thing." Randy Frame, "Sexuality Report Draws Fire," *Christianity Today* 35:5 (April 29, 1991) 37.

Appendix:
Acts 25:11 and God's Law

Dennis Johnson, of Westminster Theological Seminary, argues against the judicial use of God's Law today. He does this partly by referring to Acts 25:11 which reads: "If then I am a wrongdoer, and have committed anything worthy of death, I do not refuse to die; but if none of those things is true of which these men accuse me, no one can hand me over to them. I appeal to Caesar."

His comments on this verse are:

> Is Paul here making a direct appeal to the Mosaic judicial laws as defining crimes that cause one to be 'deserving of death'? Certainly Paul does claim not to have violated the law of the Jews (v. 8), but it is pressing his words further than the context will allow to argue that Paul expects the pagan Festus to understand the complexities of the Torah . . . well enough to find Paul's appeal intelligible and persuasive. On this point it is most natural to suppose that Paul is appealing to Roman law.[1]

Johnson errs here. Numerous and compelling indications demand that the *Mosaic* sanctions are in Paul's mind as he utters the words of Acts 25:11.

First, though Paul himself is in Caesarea, this portion of his series of trials was initially engaged before the *Sanhedrin* and Festus *by Jews* in *Jerusalem* (Acts 25:1–2). These accusers demanded that Paul be brought to Jerusalem for trial (v. 3). Thus, its historical circumstances were pre-eminently in terms of Jewish legal concerns.

Second, according to J. A. Alexander's comments on Acts 25:7, "the nature of these charges may be gathered from the former accusation [Acts 24:5–6] and the abstract of Paul's answer in the next verse."[2] The "former accusation" is found in Acts 24:5–6, where the charges before Felix read: "For we have found this man a plague, a creator of dissension among all the Jews throughout the world, and a ringleader of the sect of

---

[1] Will S. Barker and W. Robert Godfrey, *Theonomy: An Informed Critique* (Grand Rapids: Zondervan, 1990), 180–81.

[2] J. A. Alexander, *The Acts of the Apostles Explained* (New York: Anson D. F. Randolph, n.d.), 2:384.

the Nazarenes. He even tried to profane the temple, and we seized him, and wanted to judge him according to our law." Indisputably these are *Jewish* charges that, in the Sanhedrin view, demand redress "according to *our law*."

The "abstract of Paul's answer" is found in Acts 25:8: "Neither against the law of the Jews, nor against the temple, nor against Caesar have I offended in anything at all." The first two foundational points of defense relate to "the law of the Jews" and the charge regarding temple desecration. And then he adds for good measure that he has not even offended Caesar's law.

Third, because of this, Festus asked Paul: "Are you willing to go up to Jerusalem and there be judged before me concerning these things?" (Acts 25:9). *The case is close to being remanded back to the Sanhedrin, where matters of Jewish law would be dealt with.*

Fourth, an earlier charge in this series of legal woes for Paul directly relates his worthiness of death to the Jewish law: "I found out that he was accused concerning questions of *their law*, but had nothing charged against him worthy of death [*axion thanatou*] or chains" (Acts 23:29). The same terminology is used by Paul in his protestation against the charges against him: "For if I am an offender, or have committed anything worthy of death [*axion thanatou*], I do not object to dying" (Acts 25:11a).

It is important to notice that Paul considers the case already to have been tried and concluded in Jerusalem before the Sanhedrin: ". . . but if there is nothing in these things of which these men accuse me, no one can deliver me to them. I appeal to Caesar" (Acts 25:11b). That is, "if such is the result of the investigation just concluded, then *I do not refuse*."[3] "These things" charged to Paul are clearly spelled out in Acts 23:28–29: "And when I wanted to know the reason they accused him, I brought him before their council. I found out that he was accused *concerning questions of their law*, but had nothing charged against him worthy of death or chains." And later in Acts 24:13 and 20, he confirms that the trial by the council (*sunhedrion*) could not establish his guilt: "Nor can they prove the things of which they now accuse me. . . . Or else let those who are here themselves say if they found any wrongdoing in me while I stood before the council." Because of the concluded proceedings Paul can say to Festus: "To the Jews I have done no wrong, *as you very well know*."

---

[3] Alexander, *Acts*, 2:388.

Fifth, Festus writes King Agrippa regarding Paul, pointing to the Jewish charges that failed to prove him guilty of a capital offense, as they themselves argued: "King Agrippa and all the men who are here present with us, you see this man about whom the *whole assembly of the Jews* petitioned me, both at Jerusalem and here, *crying out* that *he was not fit to live any longer*" (Acts 25:24). His entire trial before the Jewish and Roman authorities reminds us of Christ's trials, wherein the Jews accused Jesus with religious charges in seeking His death: "We have a law, and according to our law He ought to die, because He made Himself the Son of God" (John 19:7).

Interestingly, in light of Johnson's complaint regarding this passage,[4] Festus admits that the Jews "had some questions against him about their own religion and about one, Jesus, who had died, whom Paul affirmed to be alive. And because I was uncertain of such questions, I asked whether he was willing to go to Jerusalem and there be judged concerning these matters" (Acts 25:20). In fact, Paul is delighted to appear before Agrippa "especially because you are expert in all customs and questions which have to do with the Jews" (Acts 26:3). He is ready to re-defend himself against "all the things of which I am accused by the Jews" (Acts 26:2).

Contrary to Johnson Acts 25:11 is relevant to the argument for the continuing validity of God's Law today and in no way hinders that argument.

---

[4] Of Acts 25:11: "it is pressing [Paul's] words further than the context will allow to argue that Paul expects the pagan Festus to understand the complexities of the Torah . . . well enough to find Paul's appeal intelligible and persuasive. On this point it is most natural to suppose that Paul is appealing to Roman law." Johnson, 181.

NOTES

NOTES

NOTES